# Prussian
# Residences

STIFTUNG
PREUSSISCHE SCHLÖSSER UND GÄRTEN
BERLIN-BRANDENBURG

Hartmut Dorgerloh · Michael Scherf

# Prussian

Royal Palaces and Gardens in Berlin and Brandenburg

# Residences

DEUTSCHER KUNSTVERLAG

# CONTENTS

# A warm welcome to the palaces and gardens of the Prussian kings!

PRUSSIA IS HISTORY: in 1918, the last Prussian king and German emperor, William II, abdicated, and in 1947, the victorious allied powers of World War II dissolved the Prussian state once and for all. Discussions about Prussia as a historical phenomenon continue to be controversial even today. When the House of Hohenzollern, a noble family originating from southern Germany, were invested with the feudal estate of the Mark Brandenburg in 1415, their rise from electors to Prussian kings and finally to German emperors was unforeseeable. On the one hand, the reasons for the continuity of the dynasty lie in its pragmatism, strengthened by Protestantism, its military strength, and its openness toward other cultures or religious influences. On the other hand, these same successful developments were bound to territorial conquests as well as to upheavals both internally and externally. Prussia's history is not fundamentally different from that of other European countries. It is more multifaceted than the black and white Prussia's coat of arms seems to suggest.

Undisputed is the outstanding significance of the palaces and gardens of the Prussian kings, which simultaneously document the eventful history of Prussia, Germany and Europe. The series of royal builders spans from Joachim II through the "Great Electors," to Frederick William, Frederick II ("the Great"), to Frederick William IV (the "Romantic on the throne") and finally to the last emperor, William II. No less impressive are the names of the architects, artists and garden designers commissioned by them, who represent the best of their age: Schlüter and Eosander, Knobelsdorff and Pesne, Schadow and Langhans, and Pückler and Schinkel. Moreover, the rich artistry of the interior decoration of the palaces is impressive, with sculptures, paintings, furniture or porcelain, thematically linking these unparalleled interior works of art with their gardens and bearing witness to the high status and political aspirations of the Prussian kings.

Berlin, and later Potsdam as a second seat of power, remained the political center of the ever growing realm. Concentrated there were the building activities of the monarchs, who regularly increased the architectural and artistic wealth of Prussia through new structures and building ensembles. The result, above all in and around Potsdam, was a network of important palace and garden complexes, whose core areas were joined together in the 19th century into an artistically designed ensemble by the great landscape gardener Peter Joseph Lenné. Since 1990, the "Palaces and Gardens in Berlin and Potsdam" have been recognized for their cultural and natural significance and placed on the UNESCO World Heritage List.

After the end of the monarchy in 1918, the Prussian state took over the palaces and gardens, which according to a contract covering the assets of the former ruling royal dynasty, transferred them to the administration of the "State Palaces and Gardens" (Staatliche Schlösser und Gärten), founded specifically for this purpose in 1927. The concept of "museum palaces" developed at that time, that the palaces and their furnishings taken together with their gardens should be preserved as historically-rooted complexes and should be made accessible to the general publi, has been in effect until today.

World War II brought about disastrous consequences for the royal residences. Bombs and fires destroyed important palaces and despite timely evacuations many works of art were lost or were taken away as war loot. The division of Germany also affected the administration of the palaces and gardens. It, too, was separated into divisions of East and West, just like the brutal Wall that after 1961 sliced through the palace and garden landscapes in both West Berlin and Potsdam. Nevertheless, despite all these difficulties, the palace administrations on both sides undertook great efforts in the restoration and preservation of the former royal buildings and grounds.

The fall of the Berlin Wall and German reunification in 1989–90 also opened new perspectives for the mutual Prussian cultural legacy. Works of art and collections could be taken out of storage and returned to their original locations, destroyed gardens could be brought back to life and important palaces in the MarkBrandenburg could be restored.

In 1995, the federal states of Berlin and Brandenburg jointly founded the "Prussian Palaces and Gardens Foundation Berlin-Brandenburg" (Stiftung Preußische Schlösser und Gärten Berlin-Brandenburg), which is also financially supported by the federal government. The foundation is responsible for the preservation, research and development of approximately 800 hectares of historic gardens and over 150 historical buildings in Berlin, Potsdam and the Mark Brandenburg. Today, all the gardens, as well as the more than 30 palaces and buildings that are represented in this book, are open to the public.

# ROYAL PALACES AND GARDENS
# IN BERLIN

The city of Berlin, which emerged in the 12th century at a flat, fordable crossing of the River Spree, was declared the permanent seat of power of the Brandenburg electors in 1486. In 1443, under the Elector Frederick II, construction began of a palace on the Island on the Spree, which would influence town planning within the city and shape the political center of Brandenburg-Prussia for nearly five centuries. The continual development of the electorate manifested itself during the 16th century in building expansions and the development of a representative Renaissance court. In 1542, the Elector Joachim II had the first palace, the Grunewald Hunting Lodge (Jagdschloss Grunewald), built outside the gates of Berlin.

The Thirty Years' War (1618–48) had a catastrophic effect upon Berlin; the court resided in the safer eastern parts of the country, trade broke down, and the total population sank by one third, to approximately 6000. The solid increase of the population to approximately 37,000 at the end of the 17th century, was a result of the calculated rebuilding and consolidation policies of the "Great Elector," Frederick William (1640–88). He moved back to Berlin with the court and began construction of a modern, urban fortification. In addition to the reorganization of the Brandenburg army, his aggressive immigration policy above all, was responsible for strengthening economic power and trade. The colonization by 5500 French citizens, the Huguenots, displaced because of their religious beliefs, considerably contributed to the city's economic success, which also led to the systematic arrangement of new city districts.

The rise from Brandenburg elector to Prussian king prompted Frederick I to begin an extensive expansion of his residence around 1700. The stately renovation and new construction of the royal Palace (Stadtschloss, 1698–1713) by Andreas Schlüter and Johann Friedrich Eosander, as well as impressive new buildings such as the Arsenal (Zeughaus, 1695–1706), Charlottenburg Palace (Lustschloss Charlotten-

burg, after 1695) and Monbijou Palace (Schloss Monbijou, 1703) for the powerful royal minister, Count von Wartenberg, document the imposing aspirations of the new kingdom, which had become a European power.

As a result of Frederick William I's concentration on the army, the proportion of military personnel in Berlin rose to more than 20% during his reign (1713–40). The Prussian kings advanced the systematic expansion of the city, which reached over 100,000 inhabitants by the middle of the 18th century. As sovereigns, however, they greatly reduced municipal rights and freedoms. Frederick II ("the Great," 1740–86) had the street "Unter den Linden" redesigned into a grand main thoroughfare, surrounded by the "Forum Fridericianum," a Roman style cluster of civic buildings, which culminated in the new opera house. Immediately following his accession to the throne, he ordered the building of the New Wing (Neuer Flügel, 1740–46) at Charlottenburg Palace, essentially completing its architectural enhancement. Afterward, his building activities concentrated more and more upon Potsdam as his secondary residence. At the end of Frederick's reign, Berlin had not only the most important German textile industry to date at its disposal, but had also established itself as the capital of a great power, influenced by the ideas of an enlightened absolutism.

Nevertheless, the Seven Years' War (1756–63), which included a brief enemy occupation of the city, had also exposed serious economic and political problems in Prussia. As these problems were never thoroughly resolved, they led to a devastating military defeat by France in 1806. As victor, Napoleon marched into the city through the Brandenburg Gate taking its crowning statue, the *Quadriga*, with him from Berlin to Paris. The triumphal return of this figural group in 1814, signified a successfully adopted political reform. Among the reforms was a strengthening of the communal responsibilities for the city of Berlin, which had been governed by municipal authorities and an assembly of municipal councilors since 1809. A broad middle-class culture also developed gradually alongside that of the court during the first half of the 19th century, whose common interests were reaffirmed in the

The Berlin Palace, central section of the east wing in the courtyard designed by Schlüter (c. 1900).

Parallel to the rise of Prussia, Berlin became the most important city in Germany after 1850, most obviously in its function as the capital of the newly founded German Reich in 1871, and the seat of power of the emperor. Before 1912, the population rose to over two million. The city expanded in all directions, bringing with it all the advantages and disadvantages of a metropolis. This rapid development ended abruptly in 1918 with the fall of the monarchy upon the loss of World War I.

At the end of 1918, revolutionary troops took over the Berlin Palace, conclusively marking the beginning of a new epoch. The incorporation of neighboring locations into the formation of greater Berlin in 1920 largely reflects the city's borders today. As a result, the growing city assimilated a number of Hohenzollern palaces and gardens which originally lay outside the city borders, and they were put to use for diverse, primarily public purposes.

The most important palaces in Berlin were badly damaged by the bombs of World War II, especially the royal Palace, which had developed over centuries into a major work of the European Baroque, but also the Monbijou, Bellevue and Charlottenburg Palaces. In contrast, those palaces which were situated more or less on the edge of the city, like the Köpenick, Grunewald or Glienicke Palaces, remained for the most part unscathed.

founding of the University (1810) and the opening of the Old Museum (Altes Museum, 1830). Urban planning developments within the seat of power experienced a clear upswing with the accession to the throne of King Frederick William IV (1840–58), a monarch passionate about architecture. The plans he had previously developed with the architect Karl Friedrich Schinkel, while still the crown prince, were to be quickly implemented: the conversion of the Pleasure Ground Wing (Lustgartenflügel, 1844–57) of the royal Palace and the construction of a distinctive cupola above the Palace Chapel (Schlosskapelle, 1845–53), the development of the Island on the Spree into a "sanctuary for the arts and sciences" (after 1841), and the new building of the Cathedral (Berliner Dom) with an extensive crypt for the Hohenzollern family (plans after 1841, but first constructed as a neo-Baroque building from 1893–1905). Growing social conflicts led to the "March Revolution" in 1848. The king fled the city for a short period, but was humbled into returning and recognizing its victims soon thereafter. As a consequence, his large-scale building projects in Berlin made slow progress.

The Baroque east wing of the Berlin Palace after World War II.

The central section of Monbijou Palace from the side facing the River Spree (1940).

The division of the city after 1945 led to confrontations between the contrasting political systems in East and West, which was also reflected in how each side dealt with the royal palaces. Although originally slated for demolition, the ruins of Charlottenburg Palace in West Berlin were eventually secured and could gradually be rebuilt. The Bellevue Palace (Schloss Bellevue, restoration 1954–59) became the official Berlin residence of the Bundespräsident, the German President.

Despite avid protest, the ruins of the Palace were blown up under the German Democratic Republic in 1950–51 to make way for parade grounds. A similar fate befell the remainder of Monbijou Palace. By contrast, Schönhausen Palace (Schloss Schönhausen) was originally used as the residence of the President of the GDR and later as a governmental guest house. In general, however, the political belief prevailed that the palaces should be torn down for the good of a new society, as relics of Prussia, which was held responsible for militarism and war. Only the main entrance of the Palace, from which Karl Liebknecht declared a soviet republic

in 1918, could be programmatically integrated into the nearby new Building of the Privy Council (Staatsratsgebäude, 1962–64) of the GDR. Equally intentional, the Palace of the Republic (Palast der Republik) was built upon a section of the former royal Palace grounds in 1973–76.

Following German Reunification in 1990, a very controversial, several-year debate about the demolition of the Palace of the Republic began in favor of reconstructing the royal Palace. After extensive sanitation and removal of asbestos, the Palace of the Republic was finally torn down by a decision of the German Bundestag in 2007–08 in order to realize the concept of the Humboldt Forum in its place. This is primarily intended to house the non-European collections of the Berlin museums, but also sections of the Berlin State Library (Landesbibliothek) and scientific collections from Humboldt University. The new building is orientated towards the old palace, of which three Baroque façades, as well as Schlüter's courtyard, are being reconstructed. Francesco Stella won the architecture competition in 2008. Completion of the Humboldt Forum is expected in 2019.

# Charlottenburg Palace and Park

Charlottenburg Palace (Schloss Charlottenburg), the largest extant Hohenzollern residence in Berlin, looks back upon an eventful 300-year history of building development and use, and through its interiors and garden architecture represents an exemplary document of the Brandenburg-Prussian reign of cultural from the late 17th to the early 20th centuries. The original building, the Lietzenburg Palace, set in the rural outskirts near what was then the Lietzow village, west of the gates of Berlin, was built from 1695–99 for Sophie Charlotte, the second wife of Elector Frederick III (later King Frederick I), according to plans designed by Johann Arnold Nering. Although the palace began with modest dimensions, a "maison de plaisance" was to be created, a summer residence in which the philosophically-inclined and musically talented Sophie Charlotte was able to gather around her an exclusive circle of artists and scholars, which, for a few years, allowed the first "court of the muses" to come to fruition in Brandenburg-Prussia. The crowning of her husband as King Frederick I of Prussia in 1701, and her own subsequently elevated stature, made extensive expansion to the palace necessary even before construction had been completed. A majestic, three-winged complex in keeping with French taste, that was designed according to plans by Johann Friedrich Eosander, was created through an extension of the longitudinal axis of the palace and through the addition of two Gentlemen's Houses (Kavalierhäuser). The formerly flat dome on the garden side of the building was shifted to the city front and raised through a tambour, or drummed cupola. The interior along the garden side of the building employed a representative enfilade – where the doors to individual rooms are aligned along a single axis – encompassing a total of 13 rooms and spanning a length of 140 meters that culminated in a room devoted to a magnificent display of porcelain. The adjacent Palace Chapel (Schlosskapelle) symbolized the close alliance between the throne and the church.

View of the Court of Honor at Charlottenburg Palace in front of the Old Palace, built by Nering and Eosander. The royal builder, Elector Frederick III, became the first king in Prussia, under the name Frederick I, in 1701.

Frederick I, Elector of Brandenburg and King in Prussia by Friedrich Wilhelm Weidemann (c. 1701).

Sophie Charlotte of Hanover, Electress of Brandenburg and Queen in Prussia by Friedrich Wilhelm Weidemann (c. 1702–05).

Of the two orangeries originally planned, only the west wing was built in 1712. Like the palace, the garden was also shaped by the Baroque style. For the palace grounds, the Frenchman Siméon Godeau created a garden on three levels after the model of Versailles, with an elongated 500 meter terrace, eight parterre de Broderie garden segments – a fashion where a garden is designed to resemble embroidery – and a carp pond imitating a harbor basin in miniature. The garden, one of the earliest Baroque designs in Germany to be based upon a French model, remained basically unchanged until after the death of Frederick the Great, in 1786.

With the early death of Sophie Charlotte in 1705, the cultural era at Lietzenburg Palace came to an end. In memory of his beloved wife, King Frederick I renamed the palace Charlottenburg. It remained his preferred secondary residence.

His successor, the "Soldier King" Frederick William I, showed no interest in the palace of his childhood, so that court life first returned with the accession to the throne of

The Porcelain Chamber forms the magnificent culmination to the showpiece chambers of Frederick I.

The Red Chamber took its name from the damask wallpaper embellished with golden braids. It is believed that Frederick I used it as a conference room.

Sophie Charlotte's "Gläsernes Schlafgemach" or mirrored bedchamber from her First Apartment.

The bedchamber of Queen Luise was arranged in 1810 according to designs by Karl Friedrich Schinkel.

The New Wing was built by Georg Wenzeslaus von Knobelsdorff for Frederick the Great from 1740–45. It replaced Rheinsberg Palace as his new residence.

The Palace Chapel, built after plans by Johann Friedrich Eosander, was consecrated in 1706. View of the altar wall.

The magnificently designed library of Frederick II, located in the First Apartment in the New Wing, faces the gardens.

Golden Gallery. This festival hall was a highlight of the Frederician interiors created for the New Wing.

his son, Frederick II, who made the palace his main seat of power. In place of the once planned eastern orangery, after 1740, Frederick had Georg Wenzeslaus von Knobelsdorff build the New Wing (Neuer Flügel) – the final architectural enhancement to the palace – lending a nearly symmetrical ground plan to the palace design. In both apartments of the New Wing, which Frederick had built until 1747 at a great expense, magnificent interior spaces like the White Hall (Weißer Saal) and the Golden Gallery (Goldene Galerie) were created that were to become highlights of the Frederician Rococo. After his move in 1747 to the newly built summer residence Sanssouci in Potsdam, Frederick only used the palace for large family celebrations. The Early Neoclassical style made its arrival in Charlottenburg Palace through Frederick II's successor, Frederick William II. In 1788, the king had five rooms on the lower level garden side of the New Wing arranged into a summer apartment in Etruscan and Chinese styles. He extended the palace with a theater and enhanced the garden with the Belvedere. In 1790, the Small Orangery (Kleine Orangerie) was added to the side facing the city. The king did not live long enough to see completion, in 1797, of the seven Winter Chambers (Winterkammern) on the upper floor of the New Wing, furnished in an Early Neoclassical style. Under Frederick William II and his successors, the Baroque garden

was gradually transformed into a landscaped English park in keeping with the taste of the times, so that very little of the original design remained. No essential changes were made to the palace during the 19th century. Frederick William III lived in a modest apartment on the main floor, while his wife Luise moved into the Winter Chambers of her father-in-law. After Luise's early death in 1810, the king had the New Pavilion (Neuer Pavillon) built in 1824–25 as a summer house for himself and his second wife. His son, Frederick William IV, resided with his wife Elisabeth on the upper floor of the Baroque central section of the building after 1841. He restored segments of the garden to an ornamental, neo-Baroque design. The last inhabitant of Charlottenburg Palace was Emperor Frederick III, during his brief, 99-day reign in 1888.

Following the end of the Hohenzollern monarchy in 1918, the building was given over to the state administration and opened for viewing in 1927. The palace was largely destroyed in 1943 during World War II, although a substantial portion of the inventory was saved from destruction by evacuation. The rebuilding of the palace carried out since the 1950s, and its reconstruction, which has been done in stages, are now being completed. The garden, completely devastated after the war, appears today in reconstructed Baroque and landscaped segments once again.

The Belvedere in the garden at Charlottenburg Palace was created for Frederick William II in 1788, by Carl Gotthard Langhans. Today, Berlin's KPM collection of porcelain is housed here.

The Prussian coronation insignia from 1701 are among the Hohenzollern royal treasures at the Old Palace.

Left:
View of Charlottenburg Palace from the gardens with the restored Baroque parterre de Broderie.

The Mausoleum, built by Heinrich Gentz in 1810, was originally intended only for the tomb of Queen Luise, created by Christian Daniel Rauch. After several expansions, it also included the sarcophagus of Frederick William III and the tombs of Emperor William I and Empress Augusta.

The New Pavilion was built in 1824–25, after plans by Karl Friedrich Schinkel, as the summer house of Frederick William III.

View of the parterre de Broderie in the palace gardens. Arranged by Siméon Godeau after 1697, it is one of the earliest Baroque gardens in Germany based on a French design.

# Schönhausen Palace

Schönhausen Palace (Schloss Schönhausen) began as an estate, which the Elector Frederick III (later King Frederick I) acquired in 1691. Together with the gardens, he subsequently had the complex expanded and decorated in a grand style by the architects Arnold Nering and Johann Friedrich Eosander.

In 1740, his grandson, Frederick the Great, transferred the palace to his wife Elisabeth Christine of Brunswick-Wolfenbüttel-Bevern, who used it as a summer residence in which she held court until her death in 1797.

The devastation of the palace during the Seven Years' War led to its extensive redesign after 1763, to which belonged a raising of the flat, side wing to the height of the three-story central section of the building, the corps de logis, and the installation of an imposing double staircase. A great many of the newly-designed rooms were decorated with precious wallpapers, hand-carved, gilded framed mirrors and ornate, decorative reliefs above the doors. Exquisite interiors were created, such as the exceptional Cedar Gallery (Zedernholzgalerie) and the Large Festival Hall (Großer Festsaal) on the top story, whose magnificent stuccowork ceiling was created by the sculptor Johann Michael Graff as a testament to the interior design of the late Frederician Rococo.

Following the death of the queen, members of the royal family only occasionally used the palace for intermittent visits, and over the course of the 19th century it became largely neglected. Peter Joseph Lenné converted the Baroque garden a into a landscaped park after 1827.

In 1920, the palace was taken over by the state administration where it served various purposes. It was used as an exhibition building and functioned as storage for so-called "Entartete Kunst" (Degenerate Art) from 1938–41. After World War II, which the palace had managed to survive practically unscathed, it was redecorated and served as the official residence of Wilhelm Pieck, the first and only president of the GDR, and from 1964–66 it was converted into a guest palace for the government.

Following extensive restoration work, Schönhausen Palace, with its 18th century interiors and redesign by the GDR government, now documents 350 years of a richly varied Prussian-German history.

The Festival Hall, an interior design from 1764, is the last originally preserved hall from the Rococo period in Berlin.

Schönhausen Palace facing the garden.

# Peacock Island

In 1794, Frederick William II, wishing to create a romantic sanctuary in keeping with fairy tales, had a small summer palace built as a picturesque, artificial ruin on Peacock Island (Pfaueninsel), which he had acquired shortly before as an expansion to the New Garden (Neuer Garten). The planning and execution were delegated to Johann Gottlieb Brendel, the court master carpenter, who erected a building with two towers and a connecting drawbridge, primarily made of wood, with the decorative frontal façade facing the New Garden. Its Early Neoclassical arrangement and furnishings, which have remained intact until today, were strongly influenced by the king's former mistress, Countess Lichtenau. The largest room was the lavishly decorated Festive Hall (Festsaal) on the upper floor, which the king used as a concert room. The monarch's effusive wanderlust found its expression in the "Otaheitische Kabinett," a Tahitian chamber, in which his longing for the idealized Tahitian island life was fused together with his own, unspoilt and wilderness-like isle. A Dairy (Meierei), in which cows were kept and a small dairy farm was operated, was built at the same time on the opposite end of the island, also as an artificial ruin and as a pendant to the palace in the neo-Gothic style. In keeping with the wish for a simple, natural life in an unspoiled landscape, the island, with its abundance of 400 old oaks, was left practically untouched. Only the areas immediately surrounding the palace and the dairy were designed into early sentimental gardens by the gardener Johann August Eyserbeck from Wörlitz, who had already contributed to the New Garden. Frederick William III, the king's son and heir, was responsible for the appearance of the island today. He used it as a rustic, remote summer residence and maintained it as a "ferme ornée," an ornamental farm. He had Peacock Island redesigned into a landscaped park by Anton Ferdinand Fintelmann and Peter Joseph Lenné, who arranged the first Prus-

The palace as seen from the water. Peacocks brought to the island, originally called "Kaninchenwerder" (Rabbit Island), coined its name.

The summer residence on Peacock Island was built as an artificial ruin at Frederick William II's behest in 1794. It was made almost exclusively of wood by the court master carpenter Johann Gottlieb Brendel.

Local wood was predominantly used for the Festival Hall on the upper floor of the palace, designed in a Neoclassical style.

sian rose garden there. A series of newly erected buildings were incorporated into the park design, including the Gentleman's Building (Kavalierhaus) in 1803–04, which was later supplied with the Gothic façade of a house from Gdańsk, and the House of Palms (Palmenhaus), built after plans by Schinkel in 1830–31, which fell victim to a fire in 1880. A Memorial Hall (Gedächtnishalle) for Queen Luise was erected in 1829. The king's fondness for all types of exotic animals led to the building of numerous menageries. The majority of the overflowing animal populations were later presented to the Berlin Zoological Garden (Zoologischer Garten) by his son and successor, Frederick William IV. With the death of Frederick William III in 1840, the artistic development of Peacock Island had reached its end.

Right:
The illusionistic wall and ceiling painting transforms the "Otaheitische Kabinett," or Tahitian chamber, into a bamboo hut. The views depicted in the faux, painted windows show the Marble Palace and the palace on Peacock Island nestled within a tropical landscape.

The Dairy was built in 1795. Its shape recreates the ruin of a Gothic church.

The artistically designed staircase in the palace's southern tower.

Right (below):
The Temple of Luise is dedicated to the memory of Queen Luise, who died in 1810. The sandstone columns came from the mausoleum in the gardens at Charlottenburg Palace, where they had been replaced by others made of red granite.

Karl Friedrich Schinkel augmented the Gentleman's Building with a late Gothic façade torn down from a patrician's house in Gdańsk.

# Glienicke Palace and Park

After his return from a trip to Italy in 1823, Prince Carl of Prussia, the third son of King Frederick William III and Queen Luise, showed interest in the Glienicke Estate, which had come up for sale. Two men, the architect Karl Friedrich Schinkel and the landscape architect Peter Joseph Lenné, had already left behind illustrations of their talents there, and their collaboration not only shaped the Glienicke Palace (Schloss Glienicke) and park, but would have an effect upon the entire cultural landscape in Potsdam as well.

The previous owner of the property, Karl August, Prince von Hardenberg, had commissioned Lenné to create a pleasure ground and Schinkel to redesign the interior. Prince Carl, who wanted to transform Glienicke into a great landscaped garden, acquired the estate on May 1, 1824 for himself and his future wife, Marie of Saxe-Weimar. Immediately following its purchase, more than a decade of continual phases of radical change took place, during which the prince was able to realize his vision of ancient Italian architecture in a charmingly Mediterranean landscape. Schinkel began by converting a building used for billiards, which was situated on the upper bank of the Havel River, into a Neoclassical summer house called the "Casino," where he created the interior decoration in a Neoclassical style and designed living and sleeping quarters for guests on the upper floor. From 1824–27, the old manor house was also rebuilt into a villa, inspired by Italian models. The private apartments of the prince and his wife, which included the newly reconstructed Red Hall (Roter Saal) and the White Salon (Weißer Salon), were placed on the upper floor. Within the palace grounds, the stable was redesigned to include a Gentleman's Wing (Kavalierflügel), behind which a tower was included to add a vertical accent to the predominantly horizontal surroundings. Pergolas, stairways and courtyards skillfully connect the building to the garden, which Lenné organized after English models into areas for flower gardens, a pleasure ground and park. The pleasure ground was provided

*Prince Carl of Prussia* (artist unknown, c. 1827).

with a series of smaller buildings, including the "Stibadium" (a covered seating area along the water), the *Lions' Fountain* (Löwenbrunnen), as well as two pavilions referred to as the Great Curiosity (Große Neugierde) and the Small Curiosity (Kleine Neugierde). Prince Carl, a passionate art collector, purchased in Italy a large quantity of fragments and sculptures from classical antiquity, which were used both to decorate the building and garden as well as to underscore the Mediterranean ambiance of the surroundings. Particularly precious objects in the collection were preserved in the "Klosterhof," a cloister-like garden pavilion, built in 1850.

After many decades of disrepair and a misappropriation of use, which followed the death of the prince in 1883, the park and buildings have been brought back to nearly the original conditions through extensive restoration and reconstruction work.

View of Glienicke Palace from the garden side with the *Lions' Fountain* (1838). Karl Friedrich Schinkel lent a Mediterranean flare to the summer residence of Prince Carl, who was greatly inspired by Italy.

The Red Hall, used as a festival hall, was the centerpiece of the interiors on the upper floor.

The Blue Corner Room was used at one time as the prince's library.

The Gentleman's Wing at the palace. Horse stables had formerly been located on the ground floor.

The garden pavilion known as the Small Curiosity was created by Schinkel in 1826 from a converted teahouse. Prince Carl later had changes made to the façade by adding a Renaissance arcade acquired in Italy.

The Great Curiosity was created as a lookout point, based upon classical edifices and Schinkel's designs.

The Stibadium, a covered seating area set before fountains that is based on a classical model, was created in 1840.

The "Klosterhof" or Cloister pavilion, built in 1850, housed important medieval and Byzantine works of art in Prince Carl's collection.

Byzantine frame enclosing a window opening on the north wall of the Cloister pavilion.

View of the Casino from the garden. Schinkel redesigned the Casino with its Neoclassical Marble Hall from a former building used for billiards in 1824–25. Guest apartments were located on the upper floor.

# Grunewald Hunting Lodge

The Grunewald Hunting Lodge (Jagdschloss Grunewald) is the oldest surviving Hohenzollern residence on Berlin soil and is at the same time a unique remnant of early Renaissance architecture in Berlin. The elector, Joachim II, Hector of Brandenburg, a ruler fond of both the arts and sciences as well as an avid hunter, had a castle built in the style of the Saxon Renaissance, amidst a remote, wild and richly-wooded terrain, called "The Green Forest" (Zum gruenen Wald). The elector himself laid the founding stone for his hunting lodge on March 7, 1542, located at the time quite far outside Berlin. Its realization was most likely carried out by the architect Caspar Theiss, and the castles in Dresden and Torgau served as its models. The original, two-story, well-fortified building was once surrounded by a large moat, over which a drawbridge led to the main gate of the castle. Used by many generations of rulers as a hunting base and for short stays, the castle went through numerous changes over the course of centuries. The most profound was its conversion in 1706 into a massive, cubed-shaped Baroque block, by the first king of Prussia, Frederick I. The building was raised, received a new roof design and larger windows. Despite these interventions, the Renaissance core of the building is recognizable even today, particularly in the octagonal tower, to which a winding staircase was added. In 1770, Frederick the Great had an adjacent building to the south remodeled into a storehouse for hunting equipment. The revival of a hunt called coursing held annually at Grunewald after 1828, which greatly increased use of the building, brought about necessary, structural improvements to the castle that had been neglected until then. Final structural changes and modernizations took place around 1900, instigated by Emperor William II. Following the end of the Hohenzollern monarchy, the castle was turned over to the state administration. The furnishings were completed and the castle was enhanced with numerous important paintings by

*The Elector Joachim II, Hector of Brandenburg* by Lucas Cranach the Younger (c. 1555).

German and Dutch artists from the 15th through the 18th centuries, including works by Lucas Cranach the Elder and by Lucas Cranach the Younger. In 1932, the building was opened to the general public as a museum. Because the castle had survived World War II largely intact, it was the first museum in Berlin able to reopen its doors, in 1949. In 1973–74, conservators reconverted the large Great Hall (Hofstube) from Joachim's era on the main floor to its original size, thus restoring to the castle an essential element of its Renaissance character. A hunting museum established in 1977 in the former Hunting Storehouse (Jagdzeugschuppen) commemorates the palace's original purpose.

View of Grunewald Hunting Lodge from the courtyard. The palace was erected as a Renaissance building in 1542 for the passionate hunter, Elector Joachim II, Hector of Brandenburg. It was redesigned using Baroque forms at the beginning of the 18th century.

Masters of the Renaissance: View into the exhibition areas displaying examples of works of art commissioned by the Brandenburg electors, including the *Cadolzburger Altar* (c. 1425/30) and Lucas Cranach the Elder's *Eve* (1537; shown in the adjacent room).

Lucas Cranach the Elder's *The Nymph of the Fountain* is one of numerous paintings in the Cranach Collection at Grunewald Hunting Lodge.

*Emperor William I's Arrival at Grunewald for the Red Hunt* by J. Arnold and H. Schnee (1887).

# ROYAL PALACES AND GARDENS
# IN POTSDAM

The Slavic settlement Poztupimi – known as Potsdam today – which was first documented in the year 993, was a small, insignificant, town in the Mark Brandenburg until after 1652, when Frederick William, the "Great Elector," developed it into his secondary seat of power after Berlin. A passionate hunter, he was enthusiastic about the abundance of game in this region that was surrounded by forest and water. The sovereign acquired the Potsdam municipal area and developed far-reaching plans for a systematic beautification of the surrounding landscape. In 1664, his friend and adviser, Johann Moritz von Nassau-Siegen, put this heroic objective into words: "The entire island must become paradise [...]."

What began at a fordable crossing above the Havel River as the conversion of a partially ruined castle into a royal Palace (Stadtschloss, after 1662, and attributed to plans by Johann Gregor Memhardt), and which included the building of a pheasant house, coach stables, orangery and pleasure gardens, so delighted the court that after 1671 it regularly stayed in Potsdam. Under the sphere of the electoral residence, the city grew, endorsed by a selective settlement of Dutch, French, Swiss and Jews. Influenced by Dutch garden and landscape design, nurseries, tree-lined streets, ornamental and vegetable gardens were created. The roots of the cultural landscape in Potsdam, which were connected to the smaller palaces built around the same time in nearby Caputh, Bornim and Glienicke, are evident here and would be extended and cultivated under the rule of the Prussian kings during the next two centuries.

Although the first Prussian king, Frederick I, concentrated upon Berlin, his successors were largely responsible for making Potsdam into a prominent location within Europe. Frederick William I turned Potsdam into a garrison town and saw to the systematic enlargement of the city, to which the "Dutch Quarter" (Holländisches Viertel, 1733–44) belongs. The new manufacturers produced their goods primarily for the growing needs of the army, which increasingly determined the street life and the character of Potsdam. Frederick II completed its development into a representative, royal seat of power. During his reign (1740–86), not only Sanssouci Palace and Park, but also 621 residential buildings, 29 factories and 99 barracks, as well as numerous public buildings were built. The king often gave exact instructions as to which Italian or English models the new architecture should be associated.

Frederick William IV ascended the throne 100 years later in 1840. Together with the renowned architect Karl Friedrich Schinkel and the brilliant landscape architect Peter Joseph Lenné, he pursued vast plans for the improvement of the entire region, which – inspired by Italy – was intended to harmoniously unify nature and art. The distinctive points of departure are represented by Sanssouci as laid out by his grandfather, the New Garden (Neuer Garten) with the Marble Palace (Marmorpalais), as well as the palaces of his brothers – Babelsberg for William (I) and Glienicke for Carl. Frederick William set new artistic heights with buildings like the Orangery Palace (Orangerieschloss) at Sanssouci, the Belvedere on the Pfingstberg, a nearby hill, or the great dome of the main city church, St. Nicholas' (Nikolaikirche). Even if some of the projects were never realized, a unique cultural landscape developed in Potsdam during the middle of the 19th century, which united the city with the royal palaces and gardens, surrounding it in a suspenseful, intertwined relationship. The newest technological achievements of the times – railroad, telegraph or steam engine buildings for the water supply of the gardens – played a significant role. The central core of these palaces and garden landscapes, which today stretch as far as the city of Berlin itself, were placed on the UNESCO World Heritage List in 1990.

During the era of the German emperors, who regularly stayed at the palaces in Potsdam, the face of the city underwent a number of further changes through an extensive array of buildings dedicated to the military, administration and to the sciences. The elite of the empire lived in villas in the new suburbs, which stretched between the various royal garden

View through the Fortuna Portal onto the courtyard of the Potsdam City Palace (c. 1912).

View of the Potsdam City Palace from the pleasure grounds (photographed in the 1930s).

developments. The generally conservative and monarchist-oriented city of Potsdam suffered greatly under the loss of its function as a seat of power in 1918, by the reduction of the army and by the economic problems of the 1920s. Before 1939, the population doubled to 136,000, through the incorporation of surrounding areas. Since 1900, a series of diverse impulses have increasingly left their marks on the city, including a continual rise in tourism, new branches of industry, like the film industry in Babelsberg, or for example the expansion of the research institutes atop the Telegrafenberg with its well-known Einstein Tower (Einsteinturm, 1920–21 by Erich Mendelsohn).

In 1933, the National Socialists staged the opening of the Reichstag as the "Day of Potsdam" in an attempt to use a Prussian tradition for their own purposes. Twelve years later, on April 14, 1945, a bombing raid destroyed a large section of the oldest part of the city, including the royal Palace. Its ruins were first demolished in 1960, as were those of the Garrison Church (Garnisonkirche) and the Church of the Holy Spirit (Heiliggeistkirche) a few years later. In the end, they fell victim to the politics of the GDR, which knowingly directed its urban planning away from Prussian history. Nevertheless, shortly after the war, during reconstruction, some attempts were made to maintain the unique Baroque structure of the

The Potsdam City Palace after World War II (1952).

city and to build upon it. After 1961, the building of the Wall destroyed a large part of the cultural landscape, and Potsdam, the regional capital since 1952, was cut off from Berlin. The royal palaces and gardens which had survived, continued to be a magnet for tourists, and have been increasingly restored since the 1970s. At about the same time, the first successful attempts to restrict the further decline of the remaining older parts of the city began to take effect. The Fall of the Berlin Wall, and the city's regained function as capital of the federal state of Brandenburg, brought about a decisive change in 1990. Nearly all the historical buildings have been renovated since then. The reconstruction of the Fortuna Por-

tal in 2002 had a signal effect for the debate about the reconstruction of the royal Palace. In 2005, it was finally decided to construct a new building for the Brandenburg State Parliament (Landtag of Brandenburg) at the same location and size of the lost palace building. However, since the results of the architectural competition for the external design were not deemed convincing, it was decided in favor of a reconstruction of the façades, which has been financed by a private donation. Numerous elements of the building decoration that were preserved before its demolition are being reintegrated into Peter Kulka's design. The building will open in 2013.

# Stern Hunting Lodge

The small Stern Hunting Lodge (Jagdschloss Stern), which was erected in 1730–32 far outside the gates of Potsdam in the style of a modest Dutch brick building, is the only palace that the "Soldier King" Frederick William I had built for himself. The king, a passionate hunter, was quite fond of coursing, popular among the European royal courts, in which the running game would be chased to the point of exhaustion by horseman and dogs and finally shot. For this purpose, the monarch had already had an enclosed Coursing Heath (Parforceheide) created in the southeast of Potsdam in 1725–29, which served as an expansive game hunting ground. From a central crossroads that functioned like a star, sixteen radially arranged open paths coursed through the flat, woodland terrain, abundant with game. These paths allowed for the unhindered pursuit of the animals. In contrast to the conventions of the times, the hunting lodge, named after its location, was not built at the center of the star, but rather a little removed from it. Behind the brick façade with a curved gable on the roof and three window axes is the main Hall (Saal), the singular official room, furnished with yellow, painted paneling, enhanced by decorative woodcarvings, paintings and animal head trophies. A tiled kitchen, an aide-de-camp's room and a bedchamber with a simple bed niche make up the rest of the space in the palace, whose functional arrangement was based on examples of middle-class home décor in Holland. The outbuildings, the palace guard's or Castellan's House (Kastellanshaus) and a stable, were carried out in a half-timbered style in keeping with local tradition.

Stern Hunting Lodge testifies not only to the middle-class taste that inspired Frederick William I, but above all, it is an expression of his high esteem for Dutch brick architecture, which he had encountered through his travels as the crown prince. After his hunting lodge was completed, the king had the Dutch Quarter (Holländisches Viertel) in Potsdam built in the same style.

The wood-paneled hall, the official room of the hunting lodge that extends through the entire length of the building, was decorated with woodcarvings and hunting trophies.

The Stern Hunting Lodge, designed as a Dutch middle-class home, is the only palace that Frederick William I had built for himself.

# Sanssouci Palace and Park

Elegantly placed to accentuate its length and seemingly untouched by the course of time, Sanssouci Palace (Schloss Sanssouci) rests upon the plateau of a vineyard. In a brief, two-year construction period, from 1745–47, the summer residence of Frederick the Great was built according to plans by the architect Georg Wenzeslaus von Knobelsdorff, drawn up from the monarch's instructions. At Frederick's behest, terraces had been laid out the year before on the "Desolate Hill" (Wüster Berg), located outside the gates of Potsdam and offering an expansive view of the magnificent landscape. Six sweeping terraces emerged within a very brief period on the southern slope of the hill. Grape vines from Italy, France and Portugal were cultivated in niches enclosed in glass, while other fruit was grown on the walls between the niches. The single-story, elongated palace building, painted in a brilliant yellow, freely modeled its design after a type of French summer residence, called the "maison de plaisance." It accommodated twelve richly furnished rooms, level with the ground, with double doors that make them directly accessible to the terraces. On the north side of the palace, two quarter circle colonnades form a Court of Honor (Ehrenhof).

Its location within a vineyard set the motif for the decorative embellishment of the palace. On the southern façade, the sculptor Friedrich Christian Glume created an arrangement of 36 paired caryatids, depicted as cheerful and drunken, Bacchus-like wine gods and goddesses, ornamented with grape foliage, who seem to be holding up the entablature. In the interior of the palace (both a work of art in itself and a major work of Frederician Rococo created by Johann August Nahl the Elder, the brothers Johann Michael Hoppenhaupt the Elder and Johann Christian Hoppenhaupt the Younger, as well as Knobelsdorff) the wine theme – and with it the connected idea of the cheerful enjoyment of life in Arcadian sur-

*Frederick the Great* by Anton Graff (c. 1781).

roundings – was also continued in the luxuriant stucco work, reliefs, sculptures and paintings.

The imposing center of the palace was formed by the magnificent Marble Hall (Marmorsaal), freely modeled upon the Pantheon in Rome according to Frederick. On special occasions Frederick II's renowned round table discussions took place here, in which the leading minds of the day participated, and whose most prominent guest was the French philosopher and Enlightenment thinker Voltaire. The Marble Hall lies across from the Vestibule (Vestibül), used as the reception hall, in which the column theme of the Court of Honor has been echoed as its design. To the east are five rooms used by Frederick, including a most luxurious Concert Room (Konzertzimmer). In this festive room, designed after the manner

Sanssouci Palace, built by Georg Wenzeslaus von Knobelsdorff in only a two-year construction period, is a major work of German Rococo architecture and was the favorite residence of Frederick the Great from 1747 until his death.

View from the colonnades across the Court of Honor to the Historic Windmill.

of a hall of mirrors and decorated with five large murals by the court painter Antoine Pesne, Frederick, a talented transverse flute musician, often acted as a soloist during the performances of his court orchestra. The rooms of the palace are placed in an enfilade, an axial suite of rooms with connecting doors. The Library (Bibliothek) in the eastern rotunda was an exception to this arrangement. Unseen and inaccessible to others, it was, with its more than 2200 volumes, a jewel encased in cedarwood paneling that was reserved as Frederick's private sanctuary. It can only be reached from the king's Bedchamber and Study (Schlaf- und Arbeitszimmer). The west wing of the palace was taken up with five guest rooms. The most prominent of these is the so-called Voltaire Room (Voltairezimmer), whose naturalistically-painted woodcarvings show motifs of exotic plants and animals. The name chosen

by Frederick the Great, "sans souci" (without a care), was intended to reflect his lifestyle. In an attempt to continue his carefree years as the crown prince at Rheinsberg, Frederick wanted to live as privately as possible at Sanssouci, far away from the royal retinue, in order to pursue his musical and philosophical inclinations, to hold his own as a "philosopher among philosophers" in profound conversations and to devote himself to his writing activities undisturbed.

For nearly four decades, Frederick the Great inhabited his Sanssouci Palace from April to October. In 1786, he died in his Bedchamber and Study. His wish to be buried in a modest tomb, which he had already had prepared on the vineyard plateau in 1744, situated alongside the graves of his whippets, was finally fulfilled on the 205th anniversary of his death in 1991. Frederick's nephew and successor to the throne, Frederick William II, had the late king's death room, which he found unsuitable, redesigned in the Early Neoclassical style by the architect Friedrich Wilhelm von Erdmannsdorff from Wörlitz.

In the same year as his accession to the throne (1840), Frederick William IV, the great-grand-nephew and the third successor to Frederick II, chose Sanssouci Palace as his summer residence. Out of respect for his formidable predecessor, he left Frederick's apartments practically untouched and instead occupied the guest rooms of the palace with his wife Elisabeth of Bavaria. In need of additional space for holding court, the sovereign instructed his architect Ludwig Persius to extend the flat service wing dating from the Frederician era. It was lengthened by two window axes, received an upper story and was adjusted to match the height of the palace. The sensitive hand of the architect is evident in the harmonious union of new and old, such that the building hardly appears to be a 19th century extension. A large Palace Kitchen was arranged in the eastern wing, while three apartments for court ladies-in-waiting were housed on the ground floor of the west wing. The upper floor was furnished with three apartments, two for gentlemen and one ladies'. In keeping with the main building, the living spaces of the Ladies' Wing (Damenflügel) were decorated in a 19th century revival style known as the "Second Rococo." Particularly noteworthy is the "Dream Room" (Traumzimmer), with its green, wood paneling and silver décor, that Persius designed in response to one of Frederick William's dreams.

Like the building of his summer residence, Frederick also continued to personally intervene in the creation and organization of the gardens, which spanned a period of more than three decades. The focus of the symmetrical arrangements is formed by a circular fountain framed by twelve marble sculptures and situated in a Baroque parterre de Broderie at the foot of the vineyard. To the west, paralleling both sides of the course of the "Hauptallee," the main avenue or promenade within the park that was laid out in a straight line which spanned from the Obelisk far into the Deer Garden (Rehgarten), was a small boscage, or copse, with trimmed bushes and trees, divided by circular flowerbeds and symmetrically arranged paths. After construction of the New Palace, which completed the Hauptallee to the West, the Deer Garden, previously designed as a landscape garden, formed the link between the newly-built palace and the pleasure garden.

The Ruinenberg, facing opposite the Court of Honor, received its name because of the decorative, ornamental buildings inspired by ancient ruins placed upon its hilltop, which

The central section of the palace with its inscription and the Bacchus-like wine gods and goddesses created by Friedrich Christian Glume.

form both a vantage point and enclose a water basin, intended to be used to supply the fountains in the park.

Like the vineyard itself, the garden was also meant to unite beauty with utility. The cultivation of fruit and vegetables for the provisions of the court played an important role. In a hedged area, primarily along the eastern side of the Hauptallee, fruit plantations with numerous trees were laid out and fruit and vegetables were cultivated in a series of hothouses and greenhouses. In 1747, an orangery was built to the west of the palace, midway up the elevation of the vineyard, for the winter storage of the valuable orange trees. It would later be redesigned into the New Chambers (Neuer Kammern).

Frederick the Great's successors had large areas of the park transformed into landscaped gardens by artists such as Johann August Eyserbeck and Peter Joseph Lenné. However the Baroque Hauptallee was left intact.

Frederick William IV was intensively involved in the preservation and expansion of Sanssouci Park. As crown prince he enriched the Frederician gardens with Charlottenhof Park to the south, designed by Lenné in the style of an English landscape garden. The king made possible the play of water, which Frederick had planned, but was never able to realize due to technical problems, and enhanced the park through smaller grounds, such as the Nordic and Sicilian Gardens, as well as the Marly Garden.

The Concert Room, a major work of the Frederician Rococo,
was the venue for the king's famous flute concerts.

Right:
Frederick the Great's legendary roundtable discussions took place
in the Marble Hall, designed by Knobelsdorff in the style of the
Pantheon in Rome.

The guestrooms, such as the Third Guestroom with its red and white wall coverings, followed a uniform scheme, but were not designed to be as stately as the rooms of the king.

Frederick the Great died in his Bedchamber and Study on August 17, 1786. His successor, Frederick William II, had the room redesigned in an early Neoclassical style that same year.

Right:
This exquisite, cedarwood paneled library, itself a work of art, was the private sanctuary of Frederick II.

Statue of *Athena with the Erichthonios Boy* in the Small Gallery. Copy of a Roman original.

Frederick had the Small Gallery installed with valuable paintings and sculptures, among which was the *Fair with Stage Players* by Antoine Watteau (c. 1715).

*The Bridal Procession* by Antoine Watteau (c. 1709) in the Small Gallery.

Details of the hand-carved wall decorations in the Voltaire Room.

The bronze sculpture of the *Praying Boy* in front of the library on the east side of the palace, which Frederick acquired in 1747, is a later cast of an original from classical antiquity.

Left:
The Voltaire Room was named for the French Enlightenment author, who stayed in Potsdam at Frederick's invitation from 1750–53.

Sanssouci Palace and Park    57

After terracing the vineyard, but before his summer palace was built, Frederick had his grave arranged in 1744. His body was finally given its final resting place here in 1991.

In the immediate vicinity of Sanssouci Palace was an adjustable windmill dating from 1738, which Frederick's successor, Frederick William II, had replaced with a Dutch windmill. A reconstruction of the windmill, which was declared a monument in 1861, but burnt down in 1945, was completed in 2003.

The Palace Kitchen with a "cooker," an early kitchen range, dating from Frederick William IV's era.

The architect Ludwig Persius designed the "Dream Room" in the Ladies' Wing after a vision in one of Frederick William IV's dreams.

The *Corradini Vase*, created by Georg Franz Ebenhech, in the western pleasure grounds.

The *Sphinx* in the central pleasure ground is also a work by the sculptor G.F. Ebenhech.

View from the Vestibule through the colonnades of the Court of Honor to the Ruinenberg. The decorative buildings imitating ancient ruins surround a reservoir, which was built to provide the water supply to the fountains in the park. The Norman Tower to the left dates to Frederick William IV's era.

Friedrich Christian Glume created eight marble sculptures for the Circle of Muses, including *Clio*, the muse of historiography.

View over the fountain pools, encircled by sculpture, through the main promenade to the New Palace.

View into the Deer Garden, located to the west of the pleasure grounds. It belongs to the landscaped park areas that Peter Joseph Lenné designed (as of 1821).

# The Picture Gallery

Frederick II's wish to have his own building devoted to the presentation of paintings and sculpture, which would also increase the importance and value of his summer residence, led to the construction of the Picture Gallery (Bildergalerie) in 1755. The location chosen was on the east side of the vineyard, a short distance below Sanssouci Palace. The building, executed by the architect Johann Gottfried Büring, was intended as a pendant to an orangery to the west, the later New Chambers (Neue Kammern). What resulted was an elongated, single-story building facing south with a prominent center section accentuated by a cupola. Eighteen marble statues symbolizing the arts and sciences were placed between the windows.

In effective contrast to the relatively simple design of the façade, the interior of the building was ornately adorned with white and yellow Italian marble, opulent gilding and sculptures. Both gallery halls and the central hall stretch practically the entire length of the building. The paintings, hung closely together in gilded frames that cover the north wall, were for the most part acquired specifically for the newly erected building. Frederick commissioned the purchase of paintings even before construction began, which as a result of Seven Years' War was drawn out until 1763. The king followed his own personal taste in the choice of the paintings. Although in his youth Frederick had, because of his preferences for contemporaneous French painters, favored Antoine Watteau and his school above all others, through mediators he now chose to purchase works from the Italian Renaissance and the Dutch and Flemish Baroque period. The king displayed a particular affinity for large-scale history paintings, highly-esteemed at the time. A smaller gallery on the east side of the building accommodates smaller paintings. When the Picture Gallery was full the king's collecting activities came to an end; in 1770, the gallery housed 168 paintings. Among the most important works are paintings such as Caravaggio's *Doubting Thomas*, *The Death of Cleopatra*

Frederick the Great's desire to create a structure for the presentation of valuable paintings and sculptures led to the construction of the Picture Gallery after 1755, the first independent museum building in Germany.

by Guido Reni and Peter Paul Rubens' *Battle of the Amazons*. The system with which Frederick had the paintings categorized was ahead of its time. Arranged by schools, the paintings of the Dutch Masters were hung in the west and center halls, while the Italian works were placed in the east wing.

In 1829, a significant part of the collection found its way into the newly established painting gallery at the Altes Museum in Berlin. The subsequent gaps were filled by paintings taken from other royal collections and through new acquisitions. This policy was also later followed to fill losses suffered during World War II. Today, the Picture Gallery is the oldest royal museum building still in use in Germany.

View into the West Hall of the Picture Gallery. In this hall, Frederick presented works of the Dutch Masters, hung closely together.

*The Garden of Love* by Peter Paul Rubens (after 1732). The painting has belonged to the Picture Gallery's inventory since 1763.

One of the major works in the Picture Gallery: Caravaggio's *Doubting Thomas*.

Frederick the Great wished to accommodate his guests within his ... y despite a limited amount of living
... ...alace. For this purpose, he had the
... the west beneath Sanssouci Palace
... ...ce. The garden building had been
... ... to plans by Georg Wenzeslaus von
... ...ter storage of valuable Mediterra-
... ...e summer months the seven empty
... ... used as event locations for balls,
... ...era performances. After two re-
... ...built for the plants, from 1771–75,
... ...ian Unger directed the renovation
... ...t palace. The exterior of the build-
... ...ged, received a cupola in keeping
... ...llery (Bildergalerie). The decora-
... ...the late Frederician Rococo style
... ...ristian Hoppenhaupt the Young-
... ...e created in the east wing, whose
... ...n increased as they progressed
... ...e Galerie) through to the main
... The Ovid Gallery (Ovidgalerie),
... ...nch precedents, was decorated
... ...ayreuth, with numerous gilded
... ...e Roman poet Ovid's *Metamor-*
... ...d lying directly at the center of
... ... functioned as a festival and
... ...(Jaspissaal), named after the
... ...h the floor and wall panels are
... ...building, for which the name
... ...ern) was soon established, is
... ...rooms and four bedrooms of
the guest area in a richly varied design, including the Green
Chamber (Grünes Lackkabinett) or the Large Intarsia Room
(Großes Intarsienkabinett) and the Small Intarsia Room
(Kleines Intarsienkabinett).

The prominent central section of the New Chambers. Beginning in
1771, Georg Christian Unger directed the conversion of an orangery
into Frederick II's guest palace.

A relief motif from the *Metamorphosis* in the Ovid Gallery:
*Jupiter and Danae.*

The apartments primarily served to accommodate high-
ranking military officials during the regularly held military
reviews and autumn maneuvers. Frederick William IV, who
chose Sanssouci Palace as his summer residence in 1840, the
same year that he ascended to the throne, had the New
Chambers renovated in 1842–43 by his architect Ludwig Persius. The building was given a colonnade on its north side and
a columned portico on its west side. In order to offer accommodations to an even greater number of guests, a loggia con-
sisting of two rooms was added to the narrow end facing
Sanssouci Palace. The living spaces of the guest wing were
hidden behind discreet alcoves in an area that had been the
servants' quarters, which were now transferred to the newly
built upper floor on the north side. Several rooms were occupied by the ladies-in-waiting of Queen Elisabeth, the consort of Frederick William IV.

The luxurious Jasper Hall is a festival hall located beneath the dome at the center of the palace.
It was named for the red, semi-precious stone, with which the walls and floor were decorated.

The Ovid Gallery was designed as a concert hall in the tradition of French mirrored halls. The Räntz Brothers, created fourteen gilded stucco reliefs after scenes from Ovid's *Metamorphosis*, one of Frederick's favorite books.

The design of the oval Buffet Hall with its centerpiece sideboard is in the Baroque tradition of a mirrored porcelain chamber.

# New Palace

Immediately following the end of the Seven Years' War, which had brought the country to the brink of ruin, Frederick the Great undertook the building of the imposing New Palace (Neues Palais). This prestigious edifice, which the monarch referred to as his "fanfaronnade," or boast, took on a symbolic character. It was meant to be a sign of the power of Prussia, which had emerged from the war victorious and with renewed strength. The design plans, in which Frederick II intervened, as he did with all of his building projects, were drawn up by Johann Gottfried Büring, who was replaced in 1765 by the appointment of the architect Carl von Gontard, from Bayreuth. A major work of late Frederician architecture, this largely Baroque, three-winged complex, with over 300 rooms that surrounded a Court of Honor (Ehrenhof), was erected within only a seven-year building period, from 1763–69. The elongated and massive façade of the two and a half-story building is structured by the protruding, central section of the building, called the corps de logis, crowned with a richly-decorated but closed cupola, and by sandstone pilasters, which connect the two main stories and the mezzanine. Small, single-story corner pavilions with cupolas, corresponding to the main building, were later added to the north and south. More than 400 sculptures, mythological figures from the sagas of antiquity and the world of the gods, decorate the façade and the roof balustrades. They are the work of a large number of sculptors, among them Johann Peter Benckert and the brothers Johann David and Johann Lorenz Wilhelm Räntz from Bayreuth. The west end of the complex is formed by the "Communs," two palatial, likewise domed utility buildings. They provided space for kitchens, utility rooms, the royal household and servants' areas, and blocked the view of the wasteland that lay behind them. The buildings, which were based on the designs of Jean Laurent Le Geay and Carl von Gontard, are connected by a semicircular colonnade, which opens to a Victory Gate (Triumphtor) at its center.

Immediately following the Seven Years' War, Frederick the Great commissioned the building of the New Palace. His "Fanfaronade," or boast, was meant to symbolize the renewed strength of Prussia.

In keeping with its function as a royal guest palace, the New Palace's builder had a series of splendidly furnished apartments created after his own designs, including the Lower Royal Suite (Unteres Fürstenquartier) and the Upper Royal Suite (Oberes Fürstenquartier), the Apartment of the Princess (Prinzessin-Wohnung) and the Apartment of Prince Henry (Heinrich-Wohnung). Johann Christian Hoppenhaupt the Younger was entrusted with furnishing the guest apartments in the late Frederician Rococo style. A vast number of artistically significant furnishings and objects were acquired or commissioned for the New Palace, including Italian and Dutch Baroque paintings, monumental ceiling paintings, porcelain and furniture. Numerous ornate pieces of furniture, ornamented with valuable inlaid work and gilded metal fittings, testify to the virtuoso skills of the cabinet makers, above all, Johann Melchior Kambly and the brothers Johann Friedrich and Heinrich Wilhelm Spindler. Particularly noteworthy are the splendidly furnished ballrooms and banqueting halls by Gontard and the galleries in the main building, the Grotto Hall (Grottensaal) and the Marble Gallery (Marmorgalerie) on the main floor, as well as the Marble Hall (Marmorsaal) and the Upper Gallery (Obere Galerie) on the top floor. In addition to the banquet and festival halls, the most significant artistic achievements are represented by the King's Apartment (Königswohnung) with its Music Room (Musikzimmer), Library (Bibliothek) and the Studies (Arbeitskabinetten), which the headstrong king had built not in the corps de logis as was in keeping with his station, but rather out of the way in the smaller of the two southern wings. The two upper floors of the larger southern wing accommodate the Palace Theater (Schlosstheater), which Johann Christian Hoppenhaupt the Younger designed in the shape of an amphitheater, with its rows placed at an incline and with gilded herm figures dividing the balcony sections that encircle the theater from one side of the proscenium to the other. Frederick the Great, who did without his own loge, had Italian operas and French dramas performed in his theater, a tradition which is continued even today.

On the garden side, the New Palace was connected to the Deer Garden (Rehgarten) through an early landscaped wood-

The palatial "Communs" housed the kitchen and other utility rooms and provided the living quarters for the servants and the royal household.

land park designed by Friedrich Zacharias Salzmann, characterized by a semicircular lawn and sculptures. The "Hauptallee," or main avenue, leading through the former hunting and game grounds and hemmed in by areas of hedges established the connection between the pleasure grounds at the bottom of the vineyard and the New Palace. From 1768–70, based upon Frederick's idea and drawn up in plans by Gontard, two domed rotundas were built in a classical style mediating between the Deer Garden and the circular lawns, imitating the corner pavilions of the New Palace. The open Temple of Friendship (Freundschaftstempel), lying to the south of the Hauptallee is dedicated to the memory of the king's favorite sister Wilhelmine of Bayreuth, who died in 1758. The northern pendant is formed by the Temple of Antiquity (Antikentempel), a small self-contained museum building, in which Frederick kept works from his collection of antiquities. Since 1921, the Temple of Antiquity has served as the mausoleum of the Empress Auguste Victoria, who died in exile in Holland.

The New Palace stood still after the death of Frederick the Great in 1786, was seldom inhabited, and occasionally served as a backdrop for festivities of the Prussian court. The palace first experienced its rediscovery after 1859, when it became the summer residence of the Crown Prince Frederick William (later Emperor Frederick III), and his wife Victoria. At the beginning of his brief, 99-day reign, the emperor renamed the palace "Schloss Friedrichskron." He died there in 1888. Restored to its old name, the New Palace was the preferred residence of Emperor William II and his wife Augusta Victoria, who lived at the palace from early spring to New Year's Day from 1889–1918. The emperor continued the modernizations which his father had begun, so that in the end the palace was equipped with baths and toilets, central heating, electricity and an elevator in the north stairwell. The main entrance of the palace was moved from the courtyard to the garden side and the terrace in front of the Grotto Hall was redesigned into a driveway ornamented with sculpture.

The impressive façade of the New Palace, Frederick II's largest palace building, spans a length of two hundred meters at the western end of the park's main promenade called the "Hauptallee."

The Grotto Hall, which faces the garden, provided official access to the King's Apartment and the guest quarters in the palace's northern section on the ground floor.

The strikingly impressive Marble Hall, designed by Gontard as the main festive hall, extends over two floors and the entire width of the central section of the building.

A showpiece of the New Palace is the King's Apartment, which Frederick had built in the southern corner pavilion at a distance from the other royal suites and festive halls. View of the Concert Room.

The study in the King's Apartment, a suite that Frederick seldom used.

This showpiece commode in the king's study, with its exquisite marquetry and silver-plated bronze ornamentation, is a work by H. W. Spindler and M. Kambly.

New Palace    75

In the northern side wing, Frederick had an apartment designed for his brother and sister-in-law, Henry and Wilhelmina. View from the Princess' Chamber into the bedchamber.

Left:
Emperor Frederick III died in the bedchamber of the Lower Royal Suite in 1888.

Right:
The installation of baths in former powder chambers or built-in closets were included among the modernizations to the New Palace. The alcove bath in the Apartment of the Prince of Prussia.

The Palace Theater at the New Palace may be counted among the few extant theaters from the 18th century in Germany. Frederick had Italian operas and French dramas performed here. View from the stage into the auditorium.

The Temple of Friendship in the Deer Garden is dedicated to the memory of Frederick's favorite sister, Wilhelmine of Bayreuth, who died in 1758.

# Chinese House and Dragon House

The cultivated fashion and fascination with China among 18th century court circles found expressions that went beyond the collection and presentation of precious Chinese luxury goods like lacquer work, silk coverings and porcelain. Asian decoration, which complied with the taste of the times in its filigree, ornamental playfulness, was immediately imitated and adopted into a formal canon of the Rococo known as "Chinoiserie." This fashion also gained an architectural resonance in the Chinese House (Chinesisches Haus) and the Dragon House (Drachenhaus) in Sanssouci Park.

The Chinese House was built by Johann Gottfried Büring according to Frederick's instructions from 1754–56, as a charming decorative garden pavilion in a secluded area, hidden at the time behind wall-high hedges, on the edge of the Deer Garden (Rehgarten). The official opening of the building was delayed by the Seven Years' War and was first celebrated with a royal banquet on April 30, 1764. The ground plan of this pavilion is shaped in the form of a cloverleaf. A circular hall in the middle of the building is attached to three mushroom-shaped chambers, which are connected to the outside through open porticos. Columns in the shape of palms at the entrances, which support the tent-like, waved roof, underscore the exotic character of the building. The elaborate, high-quality, figural decorations that surround the building were created by Johann Peter Benckert and Johann Gottlieb Heymüller. These life-size gilded sandstone statues represent cheerful Chinese figures making music or assembled together in small groups shown eating and drinking tea. Enthroned upon a tambour, or drummed cupola, sits a mandarin with an open parasol created by Benjamin Giese. The main hall was decorated with an imaginative illusionistic mural by Thomas Huber, which depicts an idealized Chinese setting of exotic birds and monkeys romping about. Today, the pavilion houses a collection of Chinese and European porcelain based on East Asian taste.

The Chinese House was created by the architect Johann Gottfried Büring as a charming backdrop for smaller court gatherings.

*The Group of Melon Eaters* is one of six figural groups, which encircle the Chinese House. They were created of gilded sandstone by Johann Peter Benckert.

The Dragon House designed by Carl von Gontard atop the Klausberg, a hill to the northwest, was built from 1770–72 in the style of a Chinese pagoda as a final bow to "Chinoiserie." Upon a closed, octagonal main story, with four concavely curved walls, rests a three-storied tower comprised of open, lantern superstructures with wooden balustrades. The 16 dragon sculptures sitting upon the folds of the roof gave the building its name. The structure, which includes a few small rooms and a kitchen, was intended to serve as the apartment of the vintner responsible for the grape vines grown on the Klausberg. However, it remained empty for a number of years, until after a restoration in 1787 when the caretaker of the Belvedere found lodging there. In the 19th century a succession of building additions were made to the Dragon House, and a restaurant has been in operation since 1934.

The Dragon House was built as "Chinoiserie," from 1770–72 by Carl von Gontard. The pagoda by William Chambers in London's Kew Gardens served as its model.

*The Violin Player*, a work by Johann Gottlieb Heymüller, is one of twelve, individual music-making statues on the Chinese House.

The building was named after the dragons on the roof of the pagoda.

Right:
The illusionistic murals and ceiling painting by Thomas Huber depicts cheerful scenery, which is populated with numerous Chinese figures, Buddhas and exotic animals.

# The Belvedere on the Klausberg

The Belvedere on the Klausberg, one of the many hills in the area, is the final building that Frederick II had erected in Sanssouci Park. This bright structure, visible from quite some distance, was constructed by the architect Georg Christian Unger in 1770–72, as the first architecturally-designed lookout point in Potsdam. Two stories rise above an elliptical ground plan, culminating in a domed roof ringed by sandstone sculptures. Both floors are encompassed by columned porticos. A free-standing double-sided staircase forms the main entrance to the building on the north side.

The interior of the Belvedere offers merely enough space for the two halls that formed a charming backdrop for smaller social gatherings. The walls and floor of the Hall (Saal) on the main floor were decorated with red jasper and white and gray marble, while the Hall on the upper floor received an oak parquet floor and jade-green marble wall panels.

The Belvedere offers a broad view over the park and the surrounding landscape. The Klausberg was incorporated into the park design of the New Palace (Neues Palais) through its lookout point and the layout of the neighboring terrain. The ridge, which borders the garden to the northeast, was once used for wine growing, and other fruit was also cultivated on numerous walls used for this purpose.

World War II left the Belvedere as a completely gutted ruin. Restoration, or rather the reconstruction of the building's exterior, began in 1990 and could be finalized in 1993. After a partial restoration of the interior, the Belvedere was opened to the public in 2003.

The hall on the upper floor with a view of the dome of the New Palace. The restored illusionistic ceiling painting by Karl Christian Wilhelm Baron and Friedrich Wilhelm Bock depicts a colorful sky animated with clouds and birds.

The Belvedere on the Klausberg was designed by Georg Christian Unger, according to instructions from Frederick II, as both a visual attraction and as a lookout point. The model was provided by Francesco Bianchini's reconstruction of Nero's emperor's palace in ancient Rome.

# Charlottenhof Palace and Park

*Frederick William IV* and *Elisabeth of Bavaria*
by Karl Wilhelm Wach (1840).

Charlottenhof Palace (Schloss Charlottenhof) is the central focus of the park named after it, which was laid out after 1826 as a southern expansion and border to the Frederician garden. It was built in 1826–29, upon the foundations of a earlier 18th century building, as the crown prince's summer residence for the future King Frederick William IV and his wife Elisabeth of Bavaria. From an older Baroque manor house, named after a previous owner, Karl Friedrich Schinkel created a small, Neo-classical villa, inspired by Italian examples from classical antiquity, which is considered to be one of the architect's main works. The artistically talented and architecturally ambitious crown prince intensively followed the planning of the building with a multitude of sketches and designs. Schinkel not only directed the building design of the palace, but also rather decisively influenced the interior design with his plans for furniture, wall decorations and other details of the interior. Upon a small ground plan, the palace housed a Vestibule (Vestibül), which extended over two floors, ten living areas on the upper floor, including the Studies (Schreibkabinette) of Frederick William and Elisabeth, a Bedchamber (Schlafzimmer) and a Living Room (Wohnzimmer), as well as two rooms for ladies-in-waiting or guests. From the official Dining Hall (Speisesaal) at the center of the palace, three double doors lead through the portico upon a terrace resting on a bank of raised earth, which is complemented to the east by an exedra, a round bench, based on a classical precedent, and to the south by a pergola entwined with vines. The small and cozy living space, whose interior has remained almost completely intact, exudes the image of a tasteful, middle-class style of living through its very private character. It was characterized by an individual color scheme, reserved décor, exquisite decorative arts and furniture. Numerous gold-framed engravings, watercolors and gouaches decorate the walls.

Repeating the collaborative design experience of the palace complex at Glienicke, the architect had a perfectly matched landscape designer, Peter Joseph Lenné, at his side. Italian models were also followed in the design of the garden grounds, formerly a flat and somewhat marshy terrain. The axial alignment from the Hippodrome (Hippodrom) through the sculpture of the *Ildefonso Group*, the Poet's Grove (Dichterhain), the terrace and through the symmetrically laid out rose garden to the man-made pond called the "Maschinenteich," make a direct reference to the main axis of the palace and incorporate it both idealistically and harmoniously into the organization of the garden grounds. Lenné designed the remaining areas in the style of an English landscape garden, with individual trees, wooded groves, defined lines of vision, effectively sculpted grounds and a sensitively arranged network of footpaths. From 1842–44, Ludwig Persius, an architect and pupil of Schinkel, added a Pheasant House (Fasanerie), which enriched the area of the park to the west.

The small, Neoclassical Charlottenhof Palace was built as a summer residence from 1826–29, according to plans by Karl Friedrich Schinkel and after designs by Crown Prince Frederick William that converted an earlier building.

The dining hall with a buffet table designed by Schinkel forms the centerpiece of the interior. Together with the vestibule, with which it is connected by a double door, it forms the main axis of the palace.

Left:
The vestibule, created from Schinkel's designs and extending over both stories of the palace, provides access to the grand living space on the upper floor.

The Tent Room was used as a bedchamber for ladies-in-waiting and guests. Schinkel modeled it after the design of Empress Josephine's Tent Room at Malmaison near Paris.

The Stibadium in the Hippodrome designed by Schinkel. This covered seating area and the geometrical arena were based on models from classical antiquity.

The rose garden arranged by Hermann Ludwig Sello in 1835 was redesigned into a flower garden in 1885 and was reconverted to its original form in 1995.

# Roman Baths

From 1829–40 the building ensemble of the Roman Baths (Römische Bäder) were created as a spiritual and aesthetic complement to the Mediterranean way of life at the nearby Charlottenhof Palace. The adaptation of the frequently altered plans by Karl Friedrich Schinkel and Crown Prince Frederick William was assigned to the architect Ludwig Persius, in whose hands the realization of the building of Charlottenhof Palace had previously been entrusted. The designs for a rustic concept which would be in contrast to the princely housing area, produced a series of varied building types divided among an asymmetrical building ensemble, that were harmoniously tied together through pergolas, arcades, gardens and arbors into a well-balanced, Mediterranean composition. Next to the Gardener's House (Gärtnerhaus), built in the style of a Tuscan villa of the 15th century, which accommodated the gardener's apartment and guest rooms, a tower on a square ground plan was added as a vertical accent, as well as a Mediterranean-inspired Staff House (Gehilfenhaus) and a Tea Pavilion (Teepavillon) in the shape of a Greek temple on a pond called the "Maschinenteich." The small, man-made pond was named after a former Steam Engine Building (Dampfmaschinenhaus) bordering the rose garden, with whose power the fountains could be operated. Behind an open Arcade Hall (Arkadenhalle), which borders the inner courtyard to the north, a bath is concealed within a replica of a Roman residential building, which gave the building ensemble its name. The Thermal Baths (Therme), designed in Pompeian style, are comprised of several rooms, including the Atrium, the Impluvium, the Apodyterium and the Caldarium. The complex is not an exact reconstruction of a Roman bath, but rather represents a free adaptation and playful variation of diverse elements of classical interior architecture that was never actually used as a thermal spring. The interior rooms were given imaginative mural paintings based on those of antiquity and were decorated with copies of classical as well as contemporary sculptures of the period.

Christian Daniel Rauch created this water-spouting flounder in 1833 using sketches by Frederick William.

The Roman Baths from the west side. The picturesque building complex was created from 1829–40 as an expression of Frederick William's enthusiasm for Italy, according to plans by Karl Friedrich Schinkel and Ludwig Persius.

View from the Atrium into the Impluvium, named after the main room of a Roman house and
a reservoir for rainwater usually sunk into the floor. Frederick William received the colossal tub
of green jasper as a gift from his brother-in-law, Czar Nicholas I.

The Caldarium, the hot water bath of the Roman thermal spring, is the main room of the baths.
The pool is sunk into the floor behind four marble caryatids.

# Steam Engine Building

The Steam Engine Building (Dampfmaschinenhaus) is a waterworks that was commissioned by Frederick William IV, erected from 1841–43 by the architect Ludwig Persius. It used a 14 piston, steam-powered pump, built by the Berlin company Borsig, which enabled the fountains in the park at Sanssouci to operate for the first time. Frederick the Great had already arranged to have a reservoir placed on the Ruinenberg, the so-called "Mount of Ruins," in order to supply the fountains in the park with rushing water at the gradient pressure of 40 meters through a downhill pipeline. The enterprise failed, however, because of the difficulty of pumping Havel River water up to that elevation. After decades of experimentation and an enormous amount of money spent in vain, in 1780, Frederick ordered that no further efforts were to made. The king had to do without the play of water and with it a central element of Baroque garden design. Frederick William IV chose a bay of the Havel as a location for the pumping station, to whose beautification it was intended to contribute. A pressure main was laid out from the engine room to the basin on the Ruinenberg and an intricate network of pipes in the park for operating the fountains. In October 1842, the largest steam engine built in Germany at that time, which could reach 81.4 horsepower, was inaugurated. After nearly 100 years, it was finally possible to fill the basin on the Ruinenberg with water from the Havel and to guarantee the continual operation of the fountains in the park. The Steam Engine Building itself was built in accordance with the predominant pluralistic styles of the day, imitating an Egyptian burial mosque with colorful bands of glazed brick, a tambour, or drummed cupola and a slender minaret as its smokestack. Even the engine room in the interior incorporated this design theme; mosques from the south of Spain served as examples in this case. Moorish arcades, which surround the steam engine as a supporting structure, combine stylistic forms of the Alhambra and the mosque in Cordoba, enhanced by orientalized stencil painting on the walls that bestow a nearly sacred atmosphere to the engine room. Today, the Steam Engine Building still provides Sanssouci Park with Havel water from the reservoir on the Ruinenberg. However, it is no longer processed through the steam engine that now forms the centerpiece of a small engineering museum, but rather through two modern, electric pumps.

Detail of the 80 horsepower steam engine, constructed by the Berlin company August Borsig. It was the first equipment powerful enough to operate the fountains in Sanssouci Park and make the play of water possible.

The pumping station, based on an Egyptian burial mosque, was built in 1841–43 by Ludwig Persius.

# Norman Tower

Frederick William IV's plans for expanding the park of Sanssouci incorporated the Ruinenberg, a neighboring hill, and the Bornstedt Fields (Bornstedter Feldflur), lying to the north. In order to pay tribute to the charm of the surrounding landscape, a four-story Norman Tower (Normannischer Turm) was built as a lookout point atop the Ruinenberg in 1846, under the direction of Ferdinand von Arnim and according to plans by Ludwig Persius. The 25 meter high tower on a square ground plan, built in the style of a medieval watchtower with a typical crown of merlon battlements or crenellations, accommodated a royal tea room, as well as an apartment in an adjoining room for the tower guard. It complemented the 18th century artificial ancient ruins that Frederick the Great had constructed after designs by Georg Wenzeslaus von Knobelsdorff and Innocente Bellavite, as a contrasting picturesque focal point in the northern extension of Sanssouci Palace's court of honor. The wall of an amphitheater, three load-bearing supporting columns with a column fragment, a rotunda and a pyramid surround a reservoir built after 1748 and later extended to operate the flow of water to the park fountains.

Even before the construction of the Norman Tower, Peter Joseph Lenné had given the Ruinenberg and the terrain situated to the north a scenic design through paths and a plantation of copses.

View from Ludwig Ferdinand Hesse's "Livestock Drinking Trough" fountain to the Ruinenberg (Mount of Ruins).

The Norman Tower on the Ruinenberg was created from designs by Ludwig Persius in 1846 as a lookout point and an enhancement to the ornamental, decorative structures built for Frederick the Great.

# The Church of Peace and the Marly Garden

The southeast border of Sanssouci Park is formed by the picturesque, Romantic building ensemble of the Church of Peace (Friedenskirche), which was built from 1845–54 by the architects Ludwig Persius and Friedrich August Stiller, according to designs by Frederick William IV and in keeping with Italian models of various epochs. The spiritual focus of the architectural design begins with the triple-nave, columned basilica, which was modeled after the early Christian church, San Clemente in Rome, and extends as far as the man-made lake, the "Friedensteich." The freestanding bell tower was based on the Roman campanile of the Church of Santa Maria in Cosmedin. In addition to the church, architectural harmony is created by a group of several adjacent cloister-like buildings, including a vicarage and schoolhouse, a gatekeeper's house and a Gentleman's Wing (Kavalierflügel). Inspired by Roman sacred architecture for its atrium and the cloisters, the ensemble was given two courtyards ringed by columns, which, like the covered colonnade along the water, were ornamented with medieval spoils of war and reliefs. Pergolas, balconies and arched corridors gracefully connect the buildings to one another. The apse of the richly-decorated church interior, fitted with various types of marble, was embellished by a unique, Italian Byzantine mosaic, made north of the Alps in the first half of the 15th century, that came from the church of San Cipriano on the island of Murano in Venice. In 1834, before the demolition of this church, Frederick William had the dimensions of the apse exactly scaled to match the size of the mosaic. In a crypt beneath the sanctuary, the royal builder and his consort, Elisabeth of Bavaria, found their final resting place.

In 1888–90, on the north side of the atrium, Julius Carl Raschdorff built a domed rotunda mausoleum for Emperor Frederick III, in which were placed the sarcophagi adorned with sculptures depicting the reposed figures of the emperor and his consort Victoria created by Reinhold Begas.

The building ensemble of the Church of Peace from the Romantic era, created in 1845–54, was based on Italian models from diverse epochs as an expression of the piety of the royal builder.

The apse mosaic from the first half of the 13th century comes from the Church of San Cipriano on the island of Murano in Venice. Frederick William acquired it during a trip to Italy and had the dome above the chancel adjusted to the measurements of the mosaic.

The gardens of the Church of Peace and the Marly Garden (Marlygarten) form the evocative, idyllic surroundings of this separate environment. With the redesign of the Marly Garden bordering to the west, the landscape gardener Peter Joseph Lenné created one of his masterpieces in a refined space. The garden had previously been laid out by the "Soldier King" Frederick William I as an austere kitchen garden, mockingly named after a magnificent garden of the French "Sun King" Louis XIV. Within a small setting, Lenné created an exemplary landscape garden, which achieved its effect through the sensitive arrangement of sculpted grounds and systematic pathways, open lawns and wooded groves, defined lines of vision, architecturally designed places to rest, and works by sculptors who were his contemporaries.

The Cloisters at the Church of Peace. The figure of *Christ* is a copy of an original by the Danish scupltor Bertel Thorvaldsen.

Heinrich Berges created the figure of the *Girl with a Parrot* that crowns a blue and white glass column.

The Mausoleum built by Julius Raschdorff, on the north side of the atrium, houses the sarcophagi of Emperor Frederick III and his wife Victoria, created by Reinhold Begas.

View through the Marly Garden to the Church of Peace.

The colonnade along the man-made lake called the "Friedensteich," created for the picturesque effect of its reflections.

The Church of Peace and the Marly Garden

# Orangery Palace

The tradition of adding royal buildings to the ensemble at Sanssouci achieved its brilliant finale with the erection of the Orangery, built upon the ridge on the northern border of the park. The plans for the structure of the Orangery Palace (Orangerieschloss) were finally realized in 1851–64, after a lengthy process that continued to be dominated by frequent alterations during the construction period. The architects Ludwig Persius, Friedrich August Stüler and Ludwig Ferdinand Hesse were obliged to closely follow the instructions of Frederick William IV, who played a significant creative role in the design of the palace. The king, for whom Italian architecture had exerted a great fascination for much of his life, found examples for the Orangery in the Roman Villa Medici and the Florentine Uffizi. From the dominant two-story central section of the building, situated around an imposing peristyle or colonnaded courtyard, loom two, tall Belvedere towers, which are also connected by a colonnade. The exceptionally long halls facing south and attached at either end, were used for the winter storage of exotic potted plants. The ensemble was completed by wide, protruding, lateral corner pavilions with large-scale passages. Located in the center of the main building is the magnificent Raphael Hall (Raffaelsaal), inspired by the Sala Regia at the Vatican, which contains copies of works of art by the Italian Renaissance artist, collected over a long period. Among the living spaces at the north, which were decorated in the 19th Century revisionist style called the "Second Rococo," and next to the Bedchamber (Schlafzimmer) and Study (Arbeitszimmer) of the king, is a guest apartment with the Malachite Room (Malachitzimmer), used by the Czarina Alexandra Feodorovna, Frederick William's sister.

The Orangery Palace is the only building executed, which was associated with Frederick William IV's plans for a "Triumphal Avenue" (Triumphstraße). The regal thoroughfare that was intended, although never built, was to be formed of a series of spectacular buildings leading from the Belvedere, high

The *Monument to Frederick William IV* erected in front of the central portal was commissioned from the sculptor Gustav Bläser in 1873, by the king's widow Elisabeth.

The monumental Orangery Palace, inspired by Italian models, was created from 1851–64 according to drawings by Frederick William IV and the plans of his architects.

Above:
The Raphael Hall (modeled on the Sala Regia at the Vatican) was built at the center of the Orangery Palace to exhibit copies of works by the Italian Renaissance master Raphael that had been assembled into a collection over many years.

Left:
A copy of Raphael's *Sistine Madonna* by Friedrich Bury.

Right (below):
Hundreds of Mediterranean potted plants are brought into winter storage in the elongated greenhouses even today.

The Malachite Room was built for Frederick William's sister, the Russian Czarina Alexandra Feodorovna, who stayed in this room during her visit in 1859.

upon the Klausberg, through the archways of the corner pavilions at the Orangery Palace, and culminating at the Triumphal Gate (Triumphtor) that was realized at the foot of the Winzerberg, east of the Picture Gallery (Bildergalerie). The king did not live long enough to see the end of construction on the terraces, which like the façade of the Orangery, were predominantly decorated with numerous sculptures of the period. His wife Elisabeth had Gustav Bläser create a marble statue to commemorate him. It was given a central position in front of the main portal. Among the garden arrangements, which were designed for the Orangery, are the Paradise Garden (Paradiesgarten) to the southwest and the Nordic Garden (Nordischer Garten) to the east, which received a contrasting counterpart in the layout of the Sicilian Garden (Sizilianischer Garten). In 1913, to mark the 25th anniversary of his accession to the throne, Emperor William II had a terrace laid out to the south of the Maulbeerallee, a main avenue. This terrace and the adjacent parterre integrate the gardens of the Orangery Palace into Sanssouci Park.

The Atrium in the Paradise Garden was built in 1845 by Ludwig Persius from sketches by Frederick William IV.

The revetment in the Sicilian Garden, once a wall used for growing fruit, was redesigned in 1862 for an installation of sculpture.

Left:
The Sicilian Garden was created from 1857–60 according to plans by Peter Joseph Lenné.

# Lindstedt Palace

In 1828, Crown Prince Frederick William (IV) acquired the Lindstedt property, an estate from the Frederician era, located to the north of the New Palace (Neues Palais), which retained the name of a previous owner. The designs for the conversion of the old manor house into a palace, which was intended to be used during his old age, came from Frederick William's own hand. The plans, whose development stretched out over decades and in which the architects Ludwig Persius, Ludwig Ferdinand Hesse, Friedrich August Stüler and Ferdinand von Arnim contributed, were finally implemented by Hesse from 1859–60. The Neoclassical villa united numerous architectural elements that were valued by the king. A long colonnaded walkway attached to the main building resembles Schinkel's Casino at Glienicke Palace, lending the asymmetrically divided complex a horizontal accent, while a round tower with a columned Belvedere provides the contrasting vertical focus. A portico and a pavilion in the form of a temple, with a staircase leading up to it, also contribute to the classical vein and Mediterranean ambiance of this small palace.

The design of the gardens and the surrounding terrain was in Lenné's domain. However, the building could no longer serve its intended purpose, because the king died at the beginning of 1861. Lindstedt Palace (Schloss Lindstedt), whose interior design has not remained intact, has experienced a full range of diverse uses since its construction and now serves as a special event and conference center.

The colonnade harmoniously connects the building with the park landscape.

Lindstedt Palace was rebuilt and expanded on the foundations of a former building as a residence for Frederick William IV in his old age. The king died, however, before construction could be completed.

# Sacrow and the Church of the Savior

Shortly after coming into power in 1840, Frederick William IV was able to further enrich the park landscape in Potsdam with the newly acquired Sacrow Estate and its accompanying park, located on the Havel River to the north of the city. In the same year, the king commissioned his architect Ludwig Persius to build a church "in the Italian style, with a campanile next to it" on the southern point of the promontory. Frederick William, himself, provided the sketches of ideas for the sacred architecture. From 1841–44, the Church of the Savior (Heilandskirche) was built with a free-standing bell tower in the architectural style of Early Christian basilicas; whereby Persius designed the lower side aisles as open colonnades encircling it. The Church of the Savior, which rises picturesquely above the Havel River, provided the lakes and park landscapes in the area with a visual focus of great charisma and attraction. Concurrently, in an accentuated site at the end of the main promenade in the park, Frederick William had a Roman bench designed after a classical model and placed next to the church, to provide a vantage point over the banks of the river.

According to Frederick William's wishes, the two-story manor house, dating from 1773, was meant to serve as the old age domicile for Friedrich Baron de la Motte Fouqué, who the king greatly admired. The poet, called to Berlin by Frederick William in 1840, had spent the happiest years of his childhood in Sacrow. However, before he could return to the site of his upbringing, Fouqué died in Berlin in 1843. As a result, Frederick William entertained the idea of converting the manor house into a medieval castle with typical merlon battlements and massive towers, in order to erect a monument to the poet and the romantically conjured, idealized world of chivalrous knights in his work. Nevertheless, the plans to convert the building, which had formally risen to the status of palace, remained unrealized.

When Frederick William IV purchased the Sacrow estate it's status rose from manor house to palace.

Around 1800, the former Late Baroque garden surrounding the building had in part already been reshaped into an earlier landscaped garden with curved paths on both sides of the old avenue called the "Kastanienallee." In order to cut costs, Lenné's plan for the garden's redesign was minimized to the cultivation of accentuating wooded areas in particularly prominent locations.

Like the New Garden (Neuer Garten) and Babelsberg Park, the banks along the river in Sacrow Park were also devastated by the construction of the Berlin Wall. The ten-year restoration of the Church of the Savior, which had fallen into decline as a result of its location on the German border, was completed in 1995. The park, marked by its direct lines of vision, historical paths and sculpted grounds, was restored to its original conditions in 1994.

The Church of the Savior, picturesquely reflected in the Havel River, was built in the shape of an Early Christian basilica by Ludwig Persius in 1840–44.

# The Marble Palace and the New Garden

One year after he took power, Frederick William II, the nephew and successor to Frederick the Great, commissioned the building of a summer palace in the New Garden (Neuer Garten) on the banks of a lake called the Heiliger See. In 1787–91, according to plans and under the direction of the architect Carl von Gontard, a virtually cubic, two-story building, crowned with a Belvedere on its flat roof was built and given the name Marble Palace (Marmorpalais), because of marble used on the façade. Carl Gotthard Langhans, commissioned to complete the design of the interior, created a wealth of Early Neoclassical interior designs for the royal builder who loved antiquity. Artists and specialists for arts and crafts, such as Heinrich Friedrich Kambly, Constantin Satori, Christian Bernhard Rode and Johann Gottfried Schadow, were entrusted with the implementation of the designs.

The interiors of the Marble Palace exemplify a décor of handcrafted furnishings, sculptures and decorative arts objects of supreme quality, including numerous ceramics from the English Wedgwood manufacturer. The architect Friedrich Wilhelm von Erdmannsdorff, from Anhalt-Dessau, served as an advisor to the royal builder. In Italy, he purchased valuable fireplaces made of Carrara marble and busts for the embellishment of the palace. The halls, side rooms and chambers were grouped symmetrically around the centrally placed Staircase Hall (Treppensaal). Among the public rooms on the ground level that faced the lake, are the Grotto Hall (Grottensaal), which was used as a dining room and the Concert Hall (Konzertsaal), while an Oriental Chamber (Orientalisches Kabinett) was placed on the upper floor. The private suites of the king were located on the main floor and included the Music Room (Musikzimmer), the Wood-Paneled Study (Boisiertes Schreibkabinett), the Dressing Room (Ankleidezimmer) and the Bedchamber (Schlafkabinett). At some distance, on the southern bank of the Heiliger See, the Gothic

*Frederick William II* by Anton Graff (1789).

Library (Gotische Bibliothek), which housed more than 1000 books, was created in historicized forms according to plans by Langhans, and a Moorish Temple (Maurisches Tempel), which has not survived, was set up as its architectural pendant on the northern bank facing opposite. The Kitchen (Küche) was also located outside the palace and connected to it by an underground passageway. It was concealed behind the façade of an artificial ruin of a Roman temple, near the Marble Palace, that appears to be sinking into the lake. Space at the Marble Palace, which was to become the favored residence of the king, soon proved to be inadequate for the needs of the royal household, and two single-story wings were added to the palace, which were connected to the main building through quarter-circle galleries – still structural

The Early Neoclassical Marble Palace, whose main building was erected on the banks of the Heiliger See from 1787–91, by Carl von Gontard and Carl Gotthard Langhans, was Frederick William II's summer palace and his preferred place of residence.

The Marble Palace from the garden side. The single-story extensions were first completed after the death of the king.

shells when the monarch died in 1797. His son and heir, Frederick William III, merely had the exterior of the building completed, but showed no further interest in his father's palace, which was to remain unused and incomplete for more than forty years. The development of the interior of the building was first carried out by Frederick William IV, according to the plans of his grandfather. Thereafter, the Marble Palace served only as an intermittent residence for royal family members. Until the completion of their own nearby Cecilienhof in 1917, Crown Prince William and his wife Cecilie were to become the last inhabitants of the Marble Palace.

The Marble Palace has been open to the public as a museum since 1932, but it suffered extreme damage during World War II. Subsequently, it was misused as an officers' club of the Red Army and then later as a military museum of the GDR. Extensive restoration and reconstruction work to both the interior and exterior have now been completed. The area along the banks of the lake, which had been destroyed by the border between the two Germanys, have also been reestablished.

The name "New Garden" signalized a breaking away from the Baroque garden design under Frederick the Great in the "old" Sanssouci Park, which for quite some time had no longer corresponded to the taste of the times. Under the direction of Johann August Eyserbeck, a gardener from Wörlitz, Frederick William II, influenced by the ideas of the Rosicrucians, commissioned a "sentimental" garden landscape with a vast number of buildings and park architecture. The asymmetrical park, made accessible by curving paths, produced its effect through irregular plantings, that made it appear overgrown and as if to be in its natural state. In small, differentiated areas of the garden, decorative and ornamental buildings, sculptures and memorial stones, richly varied and evocative in the sentimental picture sequence they offered, appealed to the senses of the viewer. Among the buildings erected were a Pyramid (Pyramide), providing access to an ice cellar, an Orangery (Orangerie) ornamented with Egyptian motifs and its lavishly decorated Hall of Palms (Palmensaal) used for concerts during the summer, a Dairy (Meierei), used for milk production within the garden premises, and a Shell Grotto (Muschelgrotte) near the lake. Servants and gentlemen of the court were lodged in houses along the so-called "Dutch Row" (Holländischen Etablissement) at the entrance to the garden. Existing residential buildings, like the Green House (Grünes Haus) and the Red House (Rotes Haus), were integrated into the design of the park, which was continually expanded through the purchase of land. After 1816, Peter Joseph Lenné eliminated the piecemeal approach to the gardens in favor of spacious, wide open areas of an English landscape garden, facilitating viewing relationships set up between the gardens and the surrounding landscape environments, so that Peacock Island (Pfaueninsel), Sacrow, Glienicke and Babelsberg became central components of the Potsdam park landscape.

The design of the vestibule is characterized by its Neoclassical reserve. It is lit through a skylight and an elegant, curved staircase leads to the rooms on the upper floor.

The Wood-Paneled Study, in which Frederick William II died in 1797.

The Concert Hall on the upper floor spans the entire length of the palace on the side facing the lake.

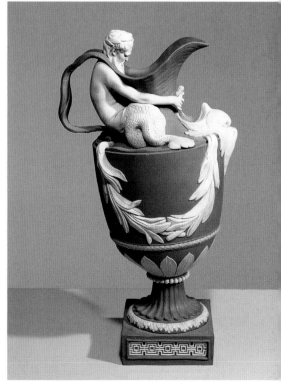

This earthenware water pitcher was produced in the English Wedgwood manufactory.

The Marble Palace and the New Garden

Upper left:
The Oriental Chamber designed as a Turkish tent by Carl Gotthard Langhans, belonged to the public rooms at the Marble Palace.

Upper right:
A gallery in the shape of a quarter circle links the main building with the southern wing. It is decorated with Pompeian-style mural paintings.

Right:
The Grotto Hall, overlooking a lake called the Heiliger See, served as a summer dining hall. It is ornamented with shells made of stucco and artificial reeds.

Like all the interiors in the southern wing, the Oval Hall is among those first created under Frederick William IV.
It was used as a festival hall and banqueting room.

The Kloeber Hall in the
northern wing is named after
the painter August von
Kloeber, who created its
mythological murals from
1845–47.

Artificial palms adorn the walls of the Hall of Palms, covered in wall panels of local wood. This room was used as a concert hall during the summer.

A statue of a sphinx decorates the Neoclassical Egyptian portal of the Orangery.

Right (below):
The Pyramid, located near the Marble Palace, provided access to an ice cellar.

The Gothic Library, built by Carl Gotthard Langhans at the southern end of the New Garden, served as a lookout tower and housed the king's book collection, which took up two floors.

The kitchens were located behind the façade of a structure imitating a Roman ruin. They were connected to the Marble Palace by an underground passageway.

# The Belvedere on the Pfingstberg and the Temple of Pomona

The towers of the Belvedere, which can be seen from quite a distance, are located west of the New Garden (Neuer Garten), high atop a hill called the Pfingstberg, providing a spectacular vantage point from the highest elevation in Potsdam, while they themselves also form an impressive viewing axis. As with many of Frederick William IV's buildings, the design plans, which matured over a decade-long process, can be traced back to the royal builder. The king found his precedents in buildings of the Italian High Renaissance, such as the Casino Caprarola located to the north of Rome.

The Belvedere, which was once intended to be a spacious palace with a view, has remained but a fragment, because the plans could only be partially completed. From 1847–52, the architects Ludwig Persius, Ludwig Ferdinand Hesse and August Stüler realized the monumental twin towered front, as well as the side enclosing walls, designed as arcades, that are crowned with colonnades. These sections of the building concealed a water reservoir located in the Inner Courtyard (Innenhof), intended to supply the cascades and fountains of the Pfingstberg building ensemble. The Belvedere became an architectural showpiece, which housed merely two artistically designed interiors in the bases of the towers used as tea rooms: the Roman Chamber (Romisches Kabinett) and the Moorish Chamber (Maurisches Kabinett). During the decade in which work on the Belvedere had ceased, the Orangery (Orangerieschloss) was built in Sanssouci Park. Frederick William IV's illness and his death in 1861 prevented the completion of the Belvedere. The planned Casino, which was to conclude in a second inner courtyard, was no longer realized, nor were the grand-scale terraces, staircases or garden arrangements, which were intended to connect the Belvedere with the New Garden. In 1863, Stüler's construction of the Entrance Hall (Eingangshalle) brought work on the Belvedere to its conclusion.

The Temple of Pomona (c. 1800) was the first work created by the 19-year-old Karl Friedrich Schinkel.

The design of the surrounding area was entrusted to Peter Joseph Lenné, who created a Neoclassical landscaped garden after 1862, in which the existing buildings were integrated. To these belonged the Temple of Pomona (Pomonatempel), built from 1800–01, and considered to be Karl Friedrich Schinkel's first work. This small pavilion at the foot of the Belvedere was commissioned by the former owner, who had used the land at that time as a vineyard. Schinkel created a cubical, temple-like building with a columned portico entrance and a lookout platform, which is accessed by a spiral staircase at the back of the building. After 1945, the Belvedere and Temple of Pomona were closed off due to their proximity to Soviet military bases and were left to fall to ruin. The reconstruction of the Temple of Pomona was completed in 1993; that of the Belvedere twelve years later.

The majestic twin towered Belvedere building complex on the Pfingstberg, created for Frederick William IV from 1847–63, crowns the highest elevation in Potsdam.

# Cecilienhof Palace

Cecilienhof Palace (Schloss Cecilienhof), in the northern sector of the New Garden (Neuer Garten), located within viewing distance of the Marble Palace (Marmorpalais), was the final palace to be built by the Hohenzollerns. Built in 1914–17 by the "Saalecker Werkstätten," a group of private designers, according to plans by the architect Paul Schultze-Naumburg, it was meant to be the permanent residence of Emperor William II's oldest son, Crown Prince William, and his wife Cecilie of Mecklenburg-Schwerin, for whom the new palace was named.

The spacious, two-story brick and half-timbered estate, whose building sections are grouped around several courtyards, adopted the architectural style of an English country house and was harmoniously integrated into the park landscape. The ground floor of the center section of the building, around which a Court of Honor (Ehrenhof) is situated, incorporated the public living space, whose unobtrusive, historicized interior architecture combined elegance with modern comfort. The English country house style was continued in the décor of the palace, which set a high standard of decorative arts throughout the interior. The centerpiece of the interior space is formed by the large, wood-paneled Living Hall (Wohnhalle), which extends over two stories. A staircase leads from here to the upper floor and to royal couple's private chambers.

After the abdication of Emperor William II, the palace was nationalized. The crown prince's family were nevertheless given a life-long right to live there, of which they availed themselves until the end of World War II.

In history, Cecilienhof achieved global importance as the site of the Potsdam Conference. From July 17 to August 2, 1945, the victorious powers of World War II used this palace to negotiate the future destiny of Germany and Europe, as no suitable locations were available in war-destroyed Berlin. The participants of the conference were Joseph W. Stalin, as founding member of the Anti-Hitler Coalition and Party

From 1914–17, during World War I, the architect Paul Schultze-Naumburg built Cecilienhof Palace in the style of an English country villa as the permanent residence of Crown Prince William.

The "Red Star," made of geraniums in the inner courtyard, was planted for the Potsdam Conference, organized by the Soviets.

Leader of the Soviet State, the British Prime Minister Winston S. Churchill, and the American President Harry S. Truman, the follower of the recently-deceased Franklin D. Roosevelt. Clement Richard Attlee replaced Churchill during the conference following the latter's election defeat. The conference, organized by the Soviets, and resulting in the so-called Potsdam Agreement, took place in the Great Hall (Große Halle) at a conference table made specifically for this purpose. The living areas of the crown prince's family were turned into working rooms for the delegation, with furniture accumulated from various palaces in Potsdam. Members of the delegation were accommodated in the numerous villas seized in Neubabelsberg. The conference rooms on the main floor have been a commemorative historical site dedicated to the Potsdam Conference since 1952.

Among Crown Princess Cecilie's interiors was a small private room, designed as a ship's cabin.

Joseph V. Stalin, Harry S. Truman and Winston S. Churchill during the proceedings at Cecilienhof Palace.

Right:
The Great Hall provided the venue for the Potsdam Conference from July 17 to August 2, 1945.

# Babelsberg Palace and Park

For more than fifty years, Babelsberg Palace (Schloss Babelsberg), picturesquely located on a slope above the Havel River, was the summer residence of the prince and later Prussian King and German Emperor William I.

The palace was built in two stages from 1834–49. The plans, which were influenced by the taste of both the royal builder and his wife, Augusta of Saxe-Weimar-Eisenach, stemmed from the hand of Karl Friedrich Schinkel. Initially, because of financial considerations, only the eastern wing could be realized, which was just one part of the entire plan, so that a cottage of modest size and well-balanced proportions in an English Neo-Gothic style was created under the direction of Ludwig Persius in 1834–35. One of the pergolas attached to the two-story eastern building established a relationship between the park and the building, the focus of which is an octagonal Dining Hall (Speisesaal) and later Tea Salon (Teesalon). In 1840, King Frederick William IV's childlessness led to his brother William's rise in status to successor to the throne. The improved financial situation and growing official needs naturally brought about proposals for the expansion of Babelsberg Palace, which went far beyond the original plans. Ludwig Persius was given the task to mediate between the architectural designs of the late Schinkel and the changing requirements of the royal builder. The architect Johann Heinrich Strack, called in upon Persius' death in 1845, completed the building of the western wing, which clearly dominated and overshadowed the older Schinkel building. The magnificent palace which emerged in the style of a Romantic castle, crowned by merlon battlements, with groups of towers and an irregular and dynamic façade, divided by buttresses, balconies, oriels and Gothic ornamentation, represents an effective contrast to Prince Carl's Mediterranean-influenced palace complex located opposite it on the Glienicke side. Under Strack's architectural and artistic direction, the palace interiors were also designed in a neo-Gothic style and augmented with historically-adapted furniture. The cen-

*Emperor William I* by Paul Bülow (1883).

ter of the palace complex is formed by the enormous octagon of the neo-Gothic Ballroom (Tanzsaal), encircled by a gallery, and culminating in star-shaped, ribbed ceiling vaults with decorations inspired by the Middle Ages. The Ballroom, and the adjacent Dining Hall designed in the Tudor style, which spans both stories, belonged to the official rooms of the new wing.

After 1833, Peter Joseph Lenné was entrusted with organizing the park into an English landscaped garden. He laid out a network of paths, which incorporated the natural charm of the hilly topography and which connected the elevations in the park with one another. As a result of the dryness caused by the then largely treeless terrain, cultivated areas were destined to only a limited success. In 1842, Prince Hermann von Pückler-Muskau replaced Lenné at Princess Augusta's

View over the pleasure ground (designed by Prince Hermann von Pückler-Muskau) onto the west wing of the palace.

The two-story Gothic Ballroom, which exudes an almost sacred character, is the main focus of the palace. Johann Heinrich Strack built it in a neo-Gothic style using designs by Ludwig Persius.

instigation. The creator of the garden arrangements at Bad Muskau and Branitz was given a large degree of artistic freedom and began by securing the park's water supply.

A Steam Engine Building (Dampfmaschinenhaus) on Glienicker Lake was built in 1843–45 according to plans by Persius. Disguised as a Norman castle, it made the irrigation of the park possible and fed into its pools, man-made lakes, waterfalls and fountains. Pückler redesigned and expanded Lenné's network of paths into narrow, cleverly guided walking paths, which led through variously designed landscaped spaces. Through a play of directed lines of vision and higher lying vantage points, myriad views were granted over the Havel River landscape and the city silhouette of Potsdam. The garden designer had lush flower arrangements created on the palace terraces and rearranged the pleasure ground laid out by his predecessor – the area of the garden in direct proximity to the palace – through sculpted grounds and what appeared to be random arrangements of sumptuously composed flowerbeds.

The park landscape was enriched through a series of buildings, medieval in appearance, placed at prominent points. The Little Palace (Kleine Schloss) on the banks of the Havel, a converted summer house built in a neo-Gothic, Tudor Revival style in 1841–42, served as the private apartment for the Crown Prince Frederick William, the later Emperor Frederick III, and subsequently as quarters for the ladies-in-waiting and guests. The Flatow Tower (Flatowturm), modeled on the tower of the Eschenheim Gate in Frankfurt am Main, was built by Strack in 1853–56 as William's private sanctuary, with both living quarters and a Belvedere lookout point. The "Sailor's Lodge" (Matrosenhaus), designed by the same architect in 1868, which imitated the stepped gables of the Stendal city hall, housed the seaman responsible for the royal boats. Finally, in 1871–72, Strack designed the "Gerichtslaube," or court pergola, upon a hill called the Lennéhöhe from segments of a 13th century building in Berlin, which had been torn down shortly before then.

The palace became neglected after the death of Emperor William I in 1888. In 1927, it came under state administration, and following World War II it was used by different institutions, each of which then altered the interiors to correspond to their varied uses. The palace interiors have been restored for museum purposes since 1990. The park, that became overgrown during the course of many decades, has been under the care of garden preservationists since 1960. The area along the water, which was destroyed to a large extent by the Berlin Wall, has been restored to its original condition.

Strack was inspired by medieval handwriting for the painted ornamention of the vaults in the Ballroom that depict foliage and music-making putto figures.

The octagonal Tea Salon, designed by Schinkel, is the point of intersection for numerous axial lines of visions both within the park and beyond it. Before the palace was expanded, it was used as the dining hall. The Tea Salon provided the basis for the ground plan of the Ballroom.

The "Sailor's Lodge" housed the seaman responsible for the royal boats. The stepped gables, created in 1868, were stylistically adapted from the medieval town hall in Stendal.

Corresponding to the Belvedere and lookout tower situated opposite it upon the Pfingstberg, the Flatow Tower was architecturally based on the tower of the Eschenheim Gate in Frankfurt am Main.

View across the pleasure ground's round flowerbed and the geyser to the Glienicke Bridge.

The "Gerichtslaube" or court pergola on the Lennéhöhe (Lenné's Hill) was built from building segments of an old city hall in Berlin, torn down around 1860.

Left (below):
The Little Palace, in a Tudor Gothic style, was created according to Augusta's instructions by converting a garden house on the banks of the Havel River. It served as the residence of Crown Prince Frederick William, and later as accomodations for ladies-in-waiting and guests.

# ROYAL PALACES AND GARDENS
# IN THE MARK BRANDENBURG

Around 1700, Frederick I commissioned the French architect Jean Baptiste Broebes, a Hugenot who had fled to Berlin, to sketch all the palaces in and around the royal seat of power and to make copper engravings of them. With a magnificent album of these architectural views, the new and first Prussian king intended to compete with the other European courts for glory and prestige. The collection of plates first appeared in 1733, and in addition to the large palaces in Berlin, Potsdam and Königsberg, it also contained numerous, smaller summer houses that had emerged in the vicinity of Berlin. The kings or members of their families used them for diverse purposes; as summer residences, or for hunting, for example. The number and conditions of the Hohenzollern palaces in the various Prussian regions changed over the course of centuries: they were bought and sold, were renovated or rebuilt, while others stood empty or were used for purposes like manufacturing. What is characteristic is their physical concentration within the Mark Brandenburg – the areas surrounding the two important seats of power in Berlin and Potsdam – as well as their exceptional artistic and architectural status.

In contrast to the nobility in other countries and courts, for instance in France or England, the nobility in Prussia was obligated and beholden to the king above all through the army or the royal administration. Noble families, who in some cases had been settled in Brandenburg for a much longer period than the Hohenzollerns, owned hundreds of palaces and manor homes in the countryside. However, only very few could hold their own against the scale and importance of the residences of the kings. The end of the monarchy in Germany in 1918, and the expropriation of the noble families in the Soviet occupied zone after 1945, literally obliterated this formerly rich, noble culture east of the Elbe. Despite the losses brought about by the war and postwar period, at least the palace buildings themselves survived in a number of locations, although they had been put to use for the most diverse purposes and were thereby frequently disfigured. Unfortunately, nothing or very little of the furnishings and interior decorations have remained intact. German reunification opened new perspectives for many of these palaces and manor homes.

In this context, the foundation that has become the Stiftung Preußische Schlösser und Gärten Berlin-Brandenburg, has taken into its care six palaces and their gardens since 1990, which are located within the Mark Brandenburg that had formed part of the landscape of the royal seat of the Prussian kings around Berlin: Rheinsberg, Oranienburg, Caputh, Königs Wusterhausen, Sacrow and Paretz. Despite the numerous changes caused by other uses, decisive features of the buildings and gardens were still extant. Some of the inventory, whether as furnishings, paintings or wallpapers, were located at other palaces or in depots. Other objects could also be relocated or repurchased.

After intensive research and accompanied by quite a few fortunate circumstances, these palaces – with the exception of Sacrow – have been refurbished and restored. They have been returned to their original historical designs as far as possible, and are now open to the public as museum palaces. Although restoration work is still continuing today, these palaces of the Mark Brandenburg are documents of the changing artistic epochs, the manifold international involvement of the Prussian kings, and the transformation of their political relationships from the 17th to the late 20th centuries.

A statue of the Roman goddess *Pomona* on the entrance portal at Rheinsberg Palace.

# Oranienburg Palace

Oranienburg Palace (Schloss Oranienburg) is the oldest extant Baroque palace in Brandenburg. In 1650, the Great Elector Frederick William transferred the rights of the title to Bötzow to his first wife Louise Henriette of Orange-Nassau. Using the walls of an old country estate, she had a palace built for herself in 1651–55, based on models of Dutch Classicism. Even before completion of the building (erected by the architect Johann Gregor Memhardt, who had completed his training in Holland) the elector gave the palace the name "Oranienburg" in his wife's honor. Shortly thereafter, the city also took on this name.

Louise Henriette's son, the Elector Frederick III and later King Frederick I, had his architects Johann Arnold Nering and Johann Friedrich Eosander redesign the palace from 1689–1711 and substantially enlarge the building through additional wings and pavilions. He completely reworked his mother's Dutch-influenced country estate and created a majestic, palace building complex influenced by Italian and French Baroque architecture. However, the gradual decline of Oranienburg Palace began with the death of Frederick I in 1713.

The palace experienced a brief and final heyday as the country estate of Prince August William, the brother of Frederick the Great, who had given him the palace in 1743 for use within his lifetime. The prince maintained it as his residence from 1744 until his early death in 1758, and had the Baroque palace interiors redesigned into the Rococo style currently in fashion.

In 1794, Crown Princess Luise received the palace as a gift from her father-in-law, Frederick William II, which however, she seldom used and only for short stays. In 1802, the neglected Oranienburg Palace was sold through the court chamberlain's offices and it endured a series of diverse uses during the 19th and 20th centuries. In quick succession, it housed a cotton factory and a chemical factory, which was

*The Elector Frederick William of Brandenburg with his first wife Louise Henriette of Orange-Nassau* by Pieter Nason (1666).

responsible for two disastrous fires, it served as a teacher's training college, a police academy and as a barracks. Severely damaged during World War II, rebuilding activities, which began in 1948, were restricted to the reconstruction of the palace's exterior.

The building was fundamentally refurbished and restored in 1997–99. Today, the municipal authorities of Oranienburg and a regional museum use the majority of the palace. Additionally, a palace museum has been housed in the reconstructed rooms laid out within the northwest wing and the central building since 2001.

Oranienburg Palace, the oldest Baroque palace complex in Brandenburg, was built by the Empress Louise Henriette of Brandenburg in 1651–55.

The étagère display of Chinese porcelain conveys an impression of the former splendor of the Porcelain Chamber, which was created from 1695–97.

The stucco ceiling decoration of the Porcelain Chamber. The painting by Augustin Terwesen, from 1697, is an allegory of the introduction of porcelain to Europe.

# Caputh Palace

The small, Baroque Caputh Palace ensemble (Schloss Caputh) is the only extant palace building from the age of the Great Electors within the Potsdam cultural landscape. The Electress Katharina had already had a country estate built for her following the acquisition of the village of Caputh in 1594. This building was later destroyed during the Thirty Years' War. In 1662, the Great Elector Frederick William gave the estate to his Superintendent of Buildings and Gardens, Philipp de Chieze, who built a simple country villa upon the foundations of the previous building.

In 1671, the elector regained the Caputh Estate and transferred its rights to his second wife Dorothea, who had the estate converted and expanded into a princely summer residence. Two square pavilion buildings were added to the south side of the building, while the north side, facing the Havel River, received a curved double-sided staircase, which led to the grand living areas on the upper floor. In the Banquet Hall (Festsaal) and the electoral couple's private apartments, magnificent interiors were fashioned with gilded stucco work and allegorical ceiling paintings, fitted with precious materials and furnishings, marble sculptures and porcelain. A multitude of paintings decorated the walls, hung closely together. The Baroque palace garden with its symmetrical segments stretched out to the banks of the Havel River.

The Elector Frederick III, son and successor to the Great Elector, presented Caputh to his second wife Sophie Charlotte, who had nevertheless created for herself, at Lietzenburg Palace (Schloss Lietzenburg), a new residence that she preferred, just outside the gates of Berlin. Caputh thus became a favorite residence of the elector, who in the meantime had been crowned king. He had the complex further developed, and in 1709 turned it into the venue of the celebrated "Meeting of Three Kings," in which he himself, the

*The Elector Frederick William of Brandenburg* and *The Electress Dorothea of Brandenburg* by Jacques Vaillant (c. 1680).

Polish King and Saxon Elector August the Strong, as well as the Danish King Frederick IV took part.

The most glorious era at Caputh ended with the death of Frederick I in 1713. His son, the "Soldier King," Frederick William I, occasionally used Caputh for hunting trips and enriched the palace around 1720 through the Tile Room (Fliesensaal), a hall completely covered with blue and white, Dutch faience tiles. Later Prussian kings showed no interest in Caputh Palace, which was leased and then sold to the von Thümen family in 1820. Shortly thereafter, under their commission, the Caputh grounds were redesigned into a landscaped garden by Peter Joseph Lenné, in which the landscape architect connected them to the Potsdam park landscapes through a footpath along the canal.

After extensive restoration work, the palace was first made accessible to the public as a museum in 1998, serving as a document of Brandenburg-Prussian architecture and the courtly style of living during the second half of the 17th century.

The Electress Dorothea turned a country villa into the summer residence at Caputh, a jewel of the royal style of living.

Caputh Palace from the south. A building addition of two corner pavilions to the square ground plan created a small Court of Honor.

The magnificently ornamented Banquet Hall, with its gilded stucco work and a ceiling painting, is the centerpiece of this small palace.

The Tile Room, in which the summer dining hall was completely covered with Dutch faience tiles, was created by Frederick William I around 1720.

Motifs showing children playing and cityscapes are typical decorations of the Dutch tiles in the Tile Room.

# Königs Wusterhausen Palace

Königs Wusterhausen Palace (Schloss Königs Wusterhausen), first mentioned in 1320, arose from a medieval castle lying at a fordable crossing of the Notte River, which over the course of centuries had passed through the possession of diverse noble families from the Mark Brandenburg. Alterations and building additions at the end of the 16th century more or less gave the well-fortified complex, previously encircled by a moat, its current form. The title to Wusterhausen came into the possession of the Hohenzollern family through the electoral prince Frederick, later King Frederick I, who had acquired it in 1683. He had the castle renovated and in part rebuilt. Baroque garden forms were designed after 1696 by the French landscape gardener Siméon Godeau, who had created the garden arrangements at Charlottenburg Palace. In 1698, the elector transferred the rights to the castle to his ten-year-old son Frederick William, the later "Soldier King" Frederick William I, with whom the place is closely associated even today.

After his accession to the throne in 1713, the monarch had the complex expanded by two Gentleman's Buildings (Kavalierhäuser). Every year, Frederick William spent the weeks between August and November with his wife Sophie Dorothea and their ten children at Königs Wusterhausen Palace, which soon became the king's preferred residence. Their stays were characterized by the hunt, which the king pursued with great passion, and by the evening social gatherings – the legendary "Tobacco Club" (Tabakskollegium) – held on a daily basis. The king, who was averse to any form of courtly pomp, led a Spartan court household and cultivated an almost "middle-class" lifestyle. The interiors of the palace rooms were correspondingly modest; they were painted in a simple whitewash and were likewise functionally furnished. Hunting trophies and paintings of hunting scenes decorated the walls, while numerous portraits of officers testified to the king's particular fondness for the military. After the death of Frederick William I in 1740, both the house and garden were neglected.

*Frederick William I* by Antoine Pesne (c. 1733)

Königs Wusterhausen Palace is closely connected with the personality of the "Soldier King," Frederick William I. Each year, he resided at the palace for several months at a time.

The rustic Festival Hall was the most official and also the largest room of the palace.

The palace experienced its rediscovery in 1855 through Frederick William IV. The renovations which he began were finalized by his brother and successor William I. After 1863, in memory of Frederick William I, the hunting tradition was once again revived at Königs Wusterhausen. It ended in 1913, in what was to be Emperor William II's final visit. After the end of the monarchy, the Prussian Palace Administration (Preußische Schlösserverwaltung) made the palace accessible as a museum in 1927. Damaged in World War II, diverse military and civil institutions used the palace for decades after the end of the war. With the completion of the restoration work in 2000, the building was reopened to the general public. Like the palace, the sections of the garden that had survived have also been restored to approximate their earlier appearances.

The "Tobacco Club." The hall was the venue for regular evening gatherings of the "Soldier King," in which the military and his envoys largely participated. Questions of state and themes concerning politics, ethics and religion were discussed in informal men's circles accompanied by copious amounts of beer and the obligatory tobacco consumption.

*The "Tobacco Club" at Königs Wusterhausen Palace,* attributed to Georg Lisiewski (c. 1737).

# Rheinsberg Palace and Park

The picturesque Rheinsberg Palace (Schloss Rheinsberg), situated on the banks of a lake called the Grienericksee, was the residence of the crown prince and later Prussian king, Frederick the Great. In 1734, the "Soldier King" Frederick William I acquired the old noble residence in the Mark Brandenburg for his son and commissioned the regional electoral superintendent of building works, Johann Gottfried Kemmeter, with the rebuilding and expansion of the small one-winged Renaissance complex. The palace wing was raised one story in order to accommodate the crown prince's apartment and the corps de logis, the central section of the building, was built upon the foundations of an old gatehouse. Upon Frederick's marriage to Elisabeth Christine of Brunswick-Wolfenbüttel-Bevern in 1736, the royal couple moved to Rheinsberg. After 1737, the master plan was shaped into a three-winged complex by the architect Georg Wenzeslaus von Knobelsdorff, who erected the north wing and the north tower, as well as a connecting colonnade. The architect also provided plans for the design of the interior. In cooperation with artists like Knobelsdorff, Friedrich Christian Glume and Antoine Pesne, Frederick developed his own concept of space that was to become the Frederician Rococo, which was implemented in an exemplary early form in the design of the Hall of Mirrors (Spiegelsaal) and later reached its flourishing height within the exquisite interiors at Sanssouci Palace (Schloss Sanssouci).

The design of the garden, which served at the same time both as a kitchen and an ornamental garden, also lay in the hands of the multi-talented Knobelsdorff, who created a geometric structure on the palace island, and to the south a symmetrical garden arrangement indebted to French garden design.

At Rheinsberg, Frederick created a "court of muses," in which, for a few years, aside from a variety of amusements,

*Prince Henry of Prussia* by Anton Graff (c. 1784–89).

he could devote himself to his philosophical, literary and musical interests. He concerned himself with the study of history, politics, with the classics and the works of French authors; and it was here that he wrote his celebrated *Anti-Machiavelli*, in which he took a stand against Machiavelli's doctrine of unscrupulous holders of power, propagating instead the position of an enlightened monarch as a servant of his country. At Rheinsberg, Frederick began his consequential correspondence with the French philosopher Voltaire. Music also played an important role in court life. The court orchestra at Rheinsberg, for which the crown prince had gathered outstanding principal musicians, was quite renowned.

Based upon his own recollections, Frederick II spent the happiest years of his life at Rheinsberg. After his accession to the throne, he transferred the rights of his crown prince's residence to his brother, Prince Henry of Prussia, who lived at the palace for fifty years, leaving his own mark on it.

The Hall of Mirrors, created by Knobelsdorff and decorated with a large ceiling painting by Antoine Pesne, has been preserved in its Frederician form.

Frederick succeeded his father to the throne in 1740. He created a new domicile for himself with the New Wing (Neuer Flügel) at Charlottenburg Palace (Schloss Charlottenburg), before he declared Sanssouci Palace (Schloss Sanssouci) as preferred residence a few years later. In 1744, the king transferred the rights to Rheinsberg Palace to his brother Henry, who moved there in 1753, following his marriage to Princess Wilhelmina of Hesse-Kassel, where he lived for nearly fifty years until he died. At first, Prince Henry left the exterior alone, but instead, took it upon himself to comprehensively rearrange the interior space. He left only five rooms in their original Frederician design, including the Hall of Mirrors (Spiegelsaal) used as a concert room, which Pesne had decorated with a large allegorical ceiling painting. The

newly designed rooms with their Late Rococo decorations, like the apartment of Princess Wilhelmina or the Shell Hall (Muschelsaal), created after 1766 according to designs by the architect Carl Gotthard Langhans, represent the transition from Late Rococo to Early Neoclassicism. Henry's final changes were made to the palace after 1785. It underwent a considerable expansion through the erection of two additional corner pavilions, both facing the city, by the architect Georg Friedrich Boumann the Younger. Henry's era saw the creation of the Long Chamber (Lange Kammer), the Master Bedchamber (Paradeschlafkammer) and the Library (Bibliothek) as new, significant interiors.

Like his brother the king, with whom he shared many of the same abilities and preferences, Henry was partial to

Based on a ground plan that once outlined four rooms, Prince Henry had Carl Gotthard Langhans design the Shell Hall. It unifies decorative elements of the Rococo and of Early Neoclassicism.

French art and culture. He continued the tradition of the "court of muses" and in 1774 had a new Palace Theater (Schlosstheater), built by Knobelsdorff with an interior in the Early Neoclassical style, erected in the western lateral wing above the former servants' quarters. The virtuoso talents of his musicians and actors, mostly of French origin, who performed several times a week, brought a brilliant reputation to the theater that extended to Berlin and beyond.

Just as the palace rooms themselves document the development from the Early Frederician Rococo to Early Neoclassicism, the garden also testifies to the changing taste of the times. Henry's rearrangement of the symmetrical Rococo garden reached its peak at the end of the century with the creation of an early landscaped garden. The prince enriched the park with a vast number of buildings, of which a few have remained, including a Fieldstone Grotto (Feldsteingrotte) and an Obelisk, set at the height of the ground-level terraces. Henry had a Pyramid Tomb (Grabpyramide) built as his final resting place. He was interred there after his death on August 3, 1802.

The radiant era at Rheinsberg ended with the death of Prince Henry in 1802. The palace remained a possession of the House of Hohenzollern until 1945, although it had been open for visitors for almost a century before. In 1950, the palace along with all of its outbuildings was turned into a sanitarium. Rheinsberg Palace, whose restoration is now complete, has been reopened to the public as a historic site since 1991.

Henry had the Master Bedchamber with its early Neoclassical design built to replace his earlier library and the Chinese Room.

Rheinsberg Palace with its Baroque garden parterres from an aerial perspective.

The library of Crown Prince Frederick was located in the circular Tower Chamber. As king, he later chose the same ground plan for his library at Sanssouci Palace.

The Long Chamber, designed in the early Neoclassical style, was created through the enlargement of the crown prince's Golden Chamber. The wall panels have remained intact.

View into the Vaulted Chamber, designed by Friedrich Reclam in 1771 to look like it dates from classical antiquity.

The Obelisk, set on the other side of the lake across from the palace, but even with its ground-level terraces, was built in 1791 in memory of Henry's brother August William and to commemorate the heroes of the Seven Years' War.

A statue of the Roman goddess *Pomona* on the palace's entrance portal.

Egeria's Grotto, named after a Roman water nymph, was created as picturesque garden architecture in 1790.

Right:
Henry had the palace island designed with a group of marble statuary and oversized wooden flower baskets, based on a French model. View towards the Obelisk.

# Paretz Palace

Paretz Palace (Schloss Paretz) was built upon the foundation walls of an old manor house in 1797, as a rural, summer retreat for Frederick William III and his wife Luise of Mecklenburg-Strelitz, by the country architect David Gilly. The rooms of this modest, well-proportioned building were designed in the Early Neoclassical style popular in Berlin, but reflecting bourgeois tastes. The Vestibule (Vestibül) and the Garden Hall (Gartensaal), as official rooms, made up the central section of the building, to which the suites with the apartments of Frederick William and Luise were attached to the east. The walls were decorated with valuable, hand-painted or printed wallpapers of the highest artistic and handcrafted quality, furnished with the finest mahogany furniture and decorative arts objects placed throughout the rooms. For the most part, the wallpaper, with its various motives and patterns, came from Berlin manufacturers.

The entire farming village was incorporated into the design of the royal residence, which was rebuilt as a classic example of Prussian bucolic architecture. The palace and the village formed an architectural ensemble and a unified work of art that provided the backdrop for the summer visits of the royal family with its large entourage, who after 1797 made annual visits, staying for several weeks during the months of August and September. Far removed from the strict Berlin court etiquette, they led an unconstrained princely life in the modest, "middle-class" ambiance of their rustic idyll. The accompanying royal household was accommodated in farmhouses and outbuildings specifically built for this purpose.

In 1806, the Napoleonic Wars forced the royal family to flee to East Prussia. After the death of Queen Luise in 1810, the king and his children regularly visited Paretz in her memory. Following Frederick William's own death in 1840, the palace was no longer inhabited, but was maintained until 1945 with its original furnishings of the era around 1800 as a commemorative site dedicated to the royal couple.

*Frederick William III and his wife Luise of Mecklenburg-Strelitz* by Friedrich Georg Weitsch (1799).

The end of World War II brought about the loss of practically the entire palace inventory, as only the valuable wallpaper could be secured in 1947. In the following years the palace underwent grave changes, including the disfigurement of the Early Classical façade and an intervention of the spatial structure by the removal of interior walls, which were altered for the sake of an agricultural institute.

The restoration of the exterior of the palace to its original state began in 1998. After the restitution of the interior, the restored wallpapers could also be returned to their original locations. Since 2001, Paretz Palace has opened its doors to the public as a museum.

Paretz Palace was built in only a few months as a country retreat for Frederick William III and his wife Luise in 1797.

The wallpaper in Queen Luise's living room was produced in 1797 by the local Berlin manufacturer Isaak Joel.
The illusionistic painting shows a view of the Marble Palace in Potsdam (on the right next to the door) and other summer landscapes.

The vestibule at Paretz Palace with oil portraits of *Frederick William III* and *Queen Luise* by Wilhelm Böttner, from 1799.

The floral motif of the wallpaper in the Garden Hall, which was used as a social room, merges together indigenous and exotic gardens.

Detail of the wallpaper in the social hall, imported from Asia.

Children's coach at the museum in the Royal Coach House at Paretz Palace (c. 1675/80).

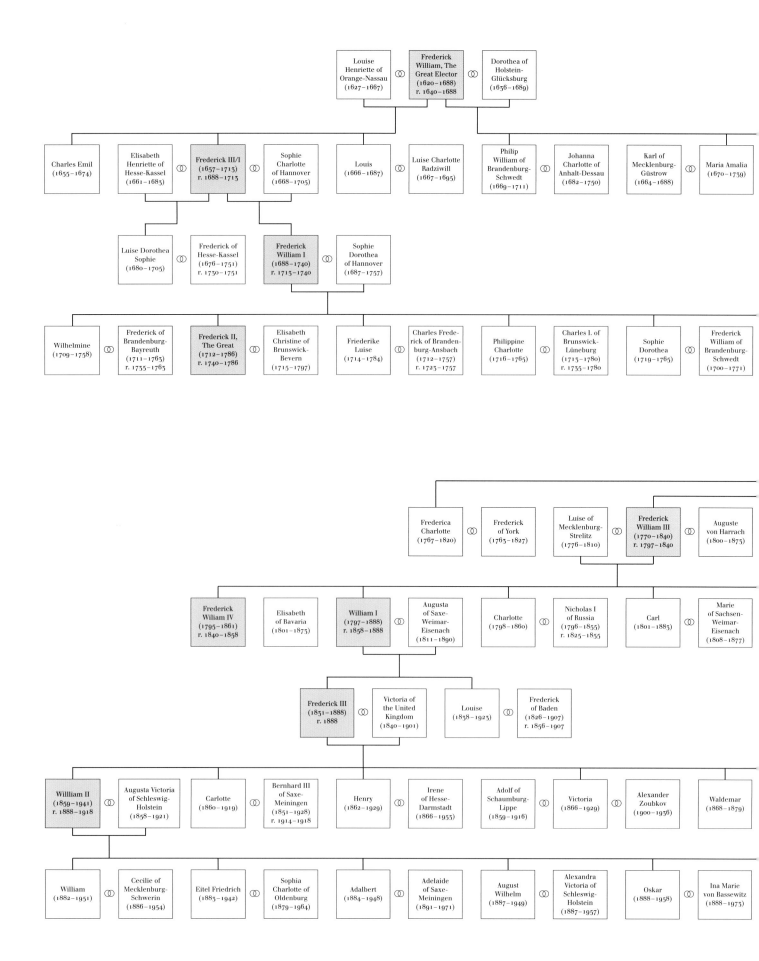

Louise
Henriette of
Orange-Nassau
(1627–1667) ⚭ **Frederick
William, The
Great Elector
(1620–1688)
r. 1640–1688** ⚭ Dorothea of
Holstein-
Glücksburg
(1656–1689)

Charles Emil
(1655–1674)

Elisabeth
Henriette of
Hesse-Kassel
(1661–1683) ⚭ **Frederick III/I
(1657–1713)
r. 1688–1713** ⚭ Sophie
Charlotte
of Hannover
(1668–1705)

Louis
(1666–1687) ⚭ Luise Charlotte
Radziwill
(1667–1695)

Philip
William of
Brandenburg-
Schwedt
(1669–1711) ⚭ Johanna
Charlotte of
Anhalt-Dessau
(1682–1750)

Karl of
Mecklenburg-
Güstrow
(1664–1688) ⚭ Maria Amalia
(1670–1739)

Luise Dorothea
Sophie
(1680–1705) ⚭ Frederick of
Hesse-Kassel
(1676–1751)
r. 1730–1751

**Frederick
William I
(1688–1740)
r. 1713–1740** ⚭ Sophie
Dorothea
of Hannover
(1687–1757)

Wilhelmine
(1709–1758) ⚭ Frederick of
Brandenburg-
Bayreuth
(1711–1763)
r. 1735–1763

**Frederick II,
The Great
(1712–1786)
r. 1740–1786** ⚭ Elisabeth
Christine of
Brunswick-
Bevern
(1715–1797)

Friederike
Luise
(1714–1784) ⚭ Charles Frederick of Branden-
burg-Ansbach
(1712–1757)
r. 1723–1757

Philippine
Charlotte
(1716–1765) ⚭ Charles I. of
Brunswick-
Lüneburg
(1713–1780)
r. 1735–1780

Sophie
Dorothea
(1719–1765) ⚭ Frederick
William of
Brandenburg-
Schwedt
(1700–1771)

Frederica
Charlotte
(1767–1820) ⚭ Frederick
of York
(1763–1827)

Luise of
Mecklenburg-
Strelitz
(1776–1810) ⚭ **Frederick
William III
(1770–1840)
r. 1797–1840** ⚭ Auguste
von Harrach
(1800–1873)

**Frederick
Wiliam IV
(1795–1861)
r. 1840–1858** ⚭ Elisabeth
of Bavaria
(1801–1873)

**William I
(1797–1888)
r. 1858–1888** ⚭ Augusta
of Saxe-
Weimar-
Eisenach
(1811–1890)

Charlotte
(1798–1860) ⚭ Nicholas I
of Russia
(1796–1855)
r. 1825–1855

Carl
(1801–1883) ⚭ Marie
of Sachsen-
Weimar-
Eisenach
(1808–1877)

**Frederick III
(1851–1888)
r. 1888** ⚭ Victoria of
the United
Kingdom
(1840–1901)

Louise
(1858–1923) ⚭ Frederick
of Baden
(1826–1907)
r. 1856–1907

**William II
(1859–1941)
r. 1888–1918** ⚭ Augusta Victoria
of Schleswig-
Holstein
(1858–1921)

Carlotte
(1860–1919) ⚭ Bernhard III
of Saxe-
Meiningen
(1851–1928)
r. 1914–1918

Henry
(1862–1929) ⚭ Irene
of Hesse-
Darmstadt
(1866–1953)

Adolf of
Schaumburg-
Lippe
(1859–1916) ⚭ Victoria
(1866–1929)

Alexander
Zoubkov
(1900–1936)

Waldemar
(1868–1879)

William
(1882–1951) ⚭ Cecilie of
Mecklenburg-
Schwerin
(1886–1954)

Eitel Friedrich
(1883–1942) ⚭ Sophia
Charlotte of
Oldenburg
(1879–1964)

Adalbert
(1884–1948) ⚭ Adelaide
of Saxe-
Meiningen
(1891–1971)

August
Wilhelm
(1887–1949) ⚭ Alexandra
Victoria of
Schleswig-
Holstein
(1887–1957)

Oskar
(1888–1958) ⚭ Ina Marie
von Bassewitz
(1888–1973)

# ROYAL LINEAGE OF THE HOUSE OF HOHENZOLLERN
## IN BRANDENBURG-PRUSSIA

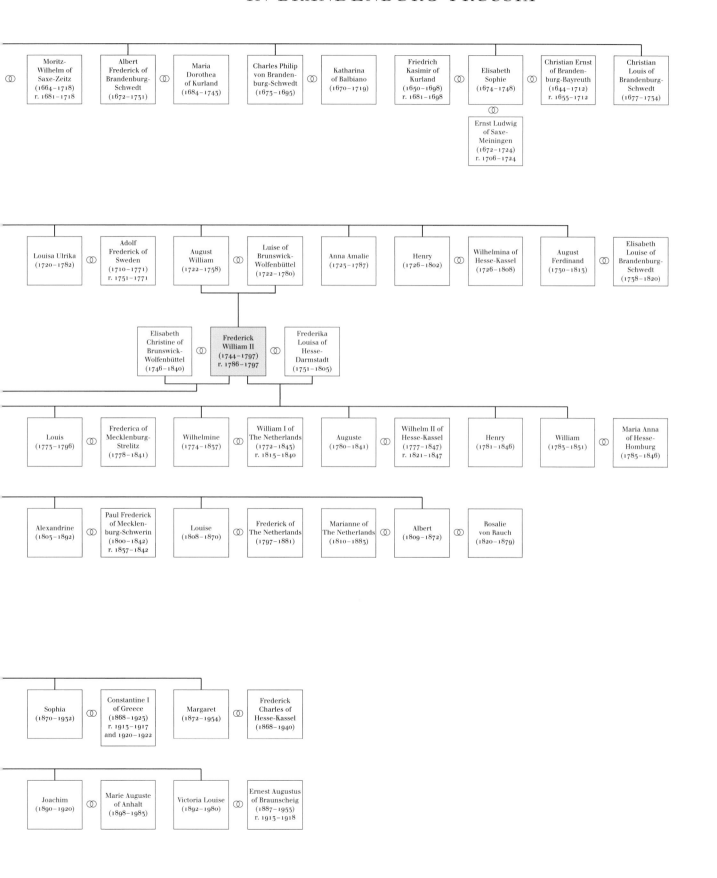

# Visitor's Information

The palace gardens are open daily
from 6:00 a.m. until dark.

Generally, all the palaces and historical buildings
represented in this book may be visited.
Several palaces are open year-round,
others only during the peak season.

**General Information.**
**Current Opening Hours and Admission Prices.**
**Special Events and Exhibitions:**

## www.spsg.de

**Visitor's Services and Information:**

Stiftung Preußische Schlösser und Gärten
Berlin-Brandenburg
Postfach 60 14 62
D-14414 Potsdam

Visitor's Center at the Historic Windmill
and at the New Palace
Am Neuen Palais 3
D-14469 Potsdam

Tel: +49 (0)331 9694 – 200
Fax: +49 (0)331 9694 – 107
e-mail: besucherzentrum@spsg.de

**Service and Group Reservations,**
**including offers for school classes and teachers:**
Tel: +49 (0)331 9694 – 200

**Museums Shop:**
www.museumsshop-im-schloss.de

**Tourist Information. Accommodations.**
**Transportation:**

in Berlin: www.visitberlin.de
in Potsdam and Brandenburg:
www.reiseland-brandenburg.de

# Imprint

**Photographic Credits:**

© Stiftung Preußische Schlösser und Gärten Berlin-
Brandenburg; Jörg P. Anders, Hans Bach, Klaus Bergmann,
Fotostudio Boettcher, Roland Bohle, Jewgeni Chaldej, Reto
Güntli, Roland Handrick, Hagen Immel, D. Katz, Daniel
Lindner, Michael Lüder, Gerhard Murza, Wolfgang Pfauder,
Leo Seidel, Barbara and René Stoltie. – Brandenburgisches
Landesamt für Denkmalpflege und Archäologisches
Landesmuseum, Messbildarchiv.

p. 2: Portal of the Orangery Palace at Sanssouci Park
(Bildarchiv SPSG/Photo: Hans Bach)
p. 4: *View of the Royal Pleasure Palace Sans Soucy near
Potsdam*, Johann David Schleuen the Elder, copperplate
engraving, c. 1747–48 (Bildarchiv SPSG/Plansammlung).
p. 6: Aerial view of Sanssouci Palace and Park
(Bildarchiv SPSG/Photo: Jürgen Hohmuth).

**Editing:**
Birgit Olbrich, Deutscher Kunstverlag

**English Translation:**
Wendy Wallis, transART, Berlin

**Production, Typesetting and Layout:**
Edgar Endl, Deutscher Kunstverlag

**Reproduction:**
Birgit Gric, Deutscher Kunstverlag

**Printing and Binding:**
Grafisches Centrum Cuno, Calbe

Bibliographical information of the Deutsche
Nationalbibliothek (German National Library)
The Deutsche Nationalbibliothek lists this publication in
the Deutsche Nationalbibliografie; detailed bibliographic
data are available on the Internet: http://dnb.dnb.de.

ISBN 978-3-422-06760-8
© 2013 Deutscher Kunstverlag GmbH Berlin München